TRAVEL
WITH
Style

ANASTASIA PASH

Master the Art of Stylish and Functional Travel Capsules

"Travel With Style"

Copyright © 2023 by Anastasia Pash

All rights reserved.

ISBN: 9798869658050

Cover Design by Matthew Davies
Photography by Yulia Yakimchuk
Book layout by Ramesh Kumar
Edited by Carmen Smith

First edition published 2023
www.travelwithstyle.co

This book is dedicated to my parents, who nurtured my sense of curiosity, love for adventure and appreciation of beauty. And to my husband, my joyful travel companion and biggest supporter. Their love has been my guiding light.

Table of Contents

Introduction

I t was disheartening to read this sentence in a travel blog. Just including it here makes me cringe: "Sneakers and even sweatpants are acceptable attire everywhere, even in upscale or fancy restaurants." What has become of us? When did travellers transform into the people always in workout gear? What happened to the days when embarking on a journey was an occasion that warranted dressing with pride?

I've travelled to more than forty countries and lived in nine across four continents. The first time I boarded a plane, I was just five years old. I still recall how elegant my mother looked whenever we travelled. She wore smart dresses and chic co-ord sets. She took great care to ensure I looked the part, too, dressing me in cute dresses, sandals, smart shorts, and T-shirts. Ironically, I thought they made me look frumpy and boring.

Growing up on a small Mediterranean island, I had already explored much of the Middle East and Europe by the time I turned seventeen. Later, I pursued my studies in the UK and completed an Erasmus exchange year at the University of Bordeaux, nestled in the enchanting heart of wine country in Southwest France. Living in the UK and France exposed me to new cultures, styles, and manners of expression. I encountered two strikingly distinct realms of style: one eclectic, scruffy, and edgy, and the other steeped in old-money aesthetics and effortless chic. This striking contrast expanded my appreciation for beauty and fashion and added depth to my own style.

After my studies, I embarked on a new chapter in bustling London, where I forged a career that offered me the privilege of travelling the world. The companies I worked for maintained a global presence, with offices scattered across Europe, Asia, and the United States. I frequently flew to fabulous destinations like New York, Paris, or Milan. I made the most of every vacation day and bank holiday, steadily accumulating stamps in my passport. I started channelling my love for travel, writing, and photography into a travel blog. What started as a hobby soon blossomed into a platform that enabled collaborations with renowned brands and granted me access to some of the world's most exclusive locations.

In 2017, I took a leap of faith, bidding farewell to the corporate world and pursuing my dreams of a more creative life. I moved to Mozambique to volunteer at a marine conservation foundation and hone my creative skills in a serene seaside village along the Indian Ocean. The three months I spent living in Africa transformed me entirely. My values shifted and so did my relationship to clothes. I began to see the absurdity of fast fashion and appreciate the value of luxury items. I commonly stumbled upon pre-loved branded pieces at local street markets in Inhambane. They landed there amongst other hand-me-downs, packed and sold by the kilo to local vendors by charitable organisations from the West. Shopping was a real treasure hunt. You never knew what you would find.

Following my stint in Africa, I moved back to Cyprus, which I used as a home base for several years. I kept travelling, blogging, and launched several businesses, all focused on travel. In late 2019, I travelled to Barcelona and didn't return to Cyprus until July 2020 because of the pandemic. Living in Barcelona during the lockdowns was an unforgettable experience that left me with many cherished friendships, photo albums full of culinary masterpieces, and enough loungewear to last a decade. During the lockdowns, we launched Globetrotter VR: a virtual travel platform that enabled grounded globetrotters to keep exploring the world from the comfort of their homes with the help of professional tour guides and virtual reality. This venture garnered international press attention, catered to thousands of virtual travellers, and got accepted into the Emirate's incubator for travel start-ups in Dubai.

The United Arab Emirates has become my new home. My family moved here in 2022, and as I compose these words, I gaze out of my window at the serene greenery of the Golden Mile Park on Palm Jumeirah. It's been a wild ride, but I am profoundly grateful for every step. My experience across diverse corners of the globe has enriched me. I appreciate that my ability to assimilate wherever I land is partly due to my cultural sensitivity and partly to my mother. She taught me at a young age that one judges a book by its cover, so you better look presentable when arriving in foreign lands. I hope that the insights I share in this book will help you have more meaningful and connecting travel experiences.

Travel is the epitome of expansion, connection, and discovery – both of the world and one-self. It's a profound experience that transcends geography, opening our hearts to the mesmerising tapestry of our world. Travel invites us to shatter the confines of our daily routines and perspectives, guiding us to embrace fresh outlooks, alternative lifestyles, and mind-boggling traditions. As Proust eloquently put it, "The true voyage of discovery consists not in seeking new landscapes, but in having new eyes." Travel is the ultimate catalyst for broadening our horizons.

While many of us pursue comfort through upgraded plane tickets, luxurious hotels, and fine dining experiences, authentic comfort runs deeper. It encompasses how we carry ourselves, express our unique identities, and navigate the complex web of culture and fashion in diverse destinations.

Throughout history, fashion has played a pivotal role in defining culture, showcasing distinctive styles, craftsmanship, and aesthetics. Consider India's intricate saris and sherwanis, which mirror the country's rich heritage and diverse regional traditions. On the other hand, the elegant kimono of Japan embodies grace, modesty, and meticulous craftsmanship. Meanwhile, in Scotland, the iconic tartan patterns serve not only as a fashion statement but also as symbols of clan affiliations and cultural pride. Fashion has always served as a medium for cultures to express individuality, preserve traditions, and foster a sense of identity.

I invite you to harness the language of clothing to communicate with the world. The workout gear and sneakers do not have to be the standard travel attire. They can be disrespectful and dismissive of cultural norms. People often resort to sportswear or jeans and T-shirts due to a lack of knowledge about what to wear. I want to transform this trend in this book.

I extend an invitation for you to become a conscious traveller and dress in a manner that respects local customs, demonstrates cultural awareness, and enables you to seamlessly integrate with the local community. It paves the way for deeper, more meaningful interactions with locals, enhancing the richness of your travel experiences.

I've packed a lot of suitcases in my travels to over forty countries in the last two decades, including European capitals, Southeast Asian islands, and African savannahs. Drawing from my extensive experiences as a passionate traveller and my collaborations with stylists and fashion experts, I have developed a methodology that guides me each time I pack. I am delighted to share it with you, empowering you to master the art of dressing with intention and ease while on the go.

In Part One, you will discover a treasure trove of inspiration and guidance for curating your travel capsule. We will explore methods for selecting outfits that align with your style and a destination's conditions. In Part Two, you will find a detailed style guide for twenty of the world's top travel destinations, plus skiing and safari adventures. Here is where you will discover summaries of the key things to consider concerning climate, comfort, and culture; recommendations on which colours, fabrics, and shoes to pack; and detailed packing lists to ensure you won't leave anything behind. In Part Three, you will find packing tips, from space-saving techniques to garment care advice for your travels. Whether you're embarking on a grand adventure spanning continents or planning a tranquil escape to a tropical paradise, this book will be your trusted guide to crafting a more thoughtful and functional travel capsule. I encourage you to read Part One thoroughly and refer to Part Two and Part Three for information and inspiration prior to your trips.

As you embark on your journey with this book, I'm eager to learn how it transforms your travel preparations and travel experiences! Please take a moment to share your insights on Amazon and

Goodreads. Your feedback is invaluable, offering fellow travellers the guidance they need when considering this book.

Join me on this stylistic voyage with an open heart and a curious mind. Together, we'll embrace the transformative power of a well-packed travel capsule. May this book help you look and feel your best wherever the road takes you!

Bon voyage!
Anastasia

Introduction

PART 1

The Art of Curating Your Travel Capsule

Chapter 1

The Three C's

Your upcoming trip is just around the corner. The excitement is palpable! You've mapped out your destination, accommodations, and even activities (more or less!). But now, you're faced with the monumental task that often induces a sense of dread: *What do I pack?*

Perhaps in the past, you've left packing until the very last day or even mere hours before heading to the airport. You'd scavenge through your wardrobe, selecting whatever clean garments you could find. Then you'd indiscriminately toss a mishmash of tops, bottoms, jeans, and dresses into your suitcase, hoping they'd serve

The Three C's

some purpose during your journey. I wager you struggled mightily to even close your suitcase because it was invariably crammed to the brim with clothing you'd never wear. We've all been there. In fact, that's precisely how I navigated most of my early twenties. On my trip to Paris for a two-week course during my studies, I lugged a suitcase that tipped the scales at over 30 kilograms. Upon arrival, I quickly discovered I hadn't packed enough warm clothing, so I needed to do emergency shopping. Bad luck for a student travelling on a budget! But here's the silver lining: There's another way! This book will unveil the art of traveling with effortless elegance without the futile attempt to squeeze your entire wardrobe into a suitcase.

Prepare to experience a paradigm shift. You're on the brink of discovering how to curate a travel capsule that's both stylish and practical. Armed with this guide, you'll never endure the torment of standing before an open suitcase, agonising over your outfit, and feeling like you've brought an excess of clothes with nothing suitable to wear.

Before you embark on your adventures, you must consider several critical factors. Think of it as a puzzle, where each piece harmoniously fits together to craft the perfect capsule. I affectionately refer to these three indispensable elements as the Three C's: Climate, Comfort, and Culture.

First and foremost, consider the climate of your chosen destination. Just as a weather vane adapts to changing weather patterns, so must your travel capsule. Equally significant is understanding the cultural sensitivities of the country you'll be exploring. It's essential to dress respectfully, avoiding attire that might inadvertently offend or draw unwarranted attention. Lastly, prioritize your comfort to ensure you can relish the activities you've planned.

Climate

Your first consideration should always be the climate of your destination. It may appear obvious, but you'd be amazed how unexpectedly hot or chilly destinations can be. Planning for specific weather conditions, especially in destinations with microclimates, will save you from the last-minute scramble to purchase suitable clothing or footwear during your trip. While impromptu holiday shopping can be enjoyable, it can also become a headache if you find yourself in a remote location with limited options. Whether you're embarking on a city break, an exotic getaway, or an adventure in the heart of nature, here's what you need to keep in mind.

Sunny Urban Getaways

If your travels lead you on a hot city in Southern Europe, coastal California, North and South Africa, Western Australia, or Western Chile, prepare for soaring temperatures, scorching sun, and fierce indoor air-conditioning.

When packing on a hot city getaway, prioritize clothing made from lightweight and breathable fabrics. Cotton, rayon, and linen allow air circulation, keeping you fresh in the sweltering heat. Opt for loose-fitting tops, dresses, and trousers to enhance airflow and ventilation. Bring along a few pairs of comfortable capri shorts or skirts suitable for a casual city setting. Pair them with lightweight tops for a laid-back look. Additionally, include a couple of sundresses or maxi dresses for an effortlessly chic appearance. Personally, I adore the combination of maxi dresses with blazers and flat sandals for a relaxed city look.

On a scorching city getaway, two essentials I never leave behind are a wide-brimmed hat and oversized sunglasses in classic black. They serve the dual purpose of protecting my face and eyes from the sun's relentless rays while adding a touch of timeless class to my outfit.

Remember that air-conditioned spaces, like restaurants or malls, tend to be quite chilly. Evenings, particularly near the coast, can also bring a lovely breeze and milder temperatures. To prepare for this, include a light cardigan, blazer, or shawl in your packing list for layering over your outfit.

Chilly Urban Getaways

When embarking on city breaks in continental destinations like Northern Europe, North America, and Asia, it's essential to be prepared for fluctuating temperatures and unpredictable weather conditions throughout the day. Layering becomes your best friend, especially when the temperatures can swing ten degrees between early morning and midday.

For winter visits to cold cities, be sure to pack essentials to ward off the chill. Include a warm coat, scarf, gloves, and hat in your luggage. I recall a winter trip to Stockholm when I neglected to bring a hat and quickly found my ears practically frozen. Fortunately, a quick dash to the local high street yielded a fabulous woollen fedora, saving the day.

In harsher conditions, make sure to include comfortable walking shoes and a pair of high-quality wool socks for added insulation, and be prepared for cobblestone streets that require sturdy footwear. These items form the foundation of your city-break attire, allowing you to craft the rest of your outfits around them.

In the summer, temperatures in these regions can rise to the low- to mid-twenties degrees Celsius. To fully savour the pleasant weather, opt for lightweight and breathable clothing. Create a mix of short-sleeved and sleeveless tops crafted from breathable materials like cotton or linen. Ensure you have several pairs of comfortable capri shorts or skirts suitable for leisurely strolls and urban exploration. Lightweight, quick-drying fabrics are ideal for your summer capsule in this climate.

Bring along a pair of jeans or long trousers for crisp evenings or cultural sites that require modest attire. Similarly, include a hoodie, sweater, or cardigan for those chilly days or evenings when temperatures drop unexpectedly. As the weather can be unpredictable, consider packing a versatile parka, a classic trench coat, and rain-resistant footwear. They will be your trusted companions. And remember to include a travel-size umbrella in your luggage for a surprise shower or two.

Regarding footwear, comfortable walking shoes or sneakers are indispensable for manoeuvring cobblestone streets and exploring the city. Ensure they offer ample cushioning for long strolls. On warmer days, sandals or open-toed shoes are an excellent choice to keep your feet fresh and comfortable while navigating the urban landscape.

Mountain Expeditions

Venturing into the mountains presents a unique packing challenge, the weather conditions in these rugged terrains shift dramatically and unexpectedly. Select clothing that offers both warmth and versatility, allowing you to adapt to changing conditions on the fly.

The key is a well-structured layering system: the base layer, mid layer, and outer layer.

Base Layer: Start with a moisture-wicking and insulating base layer made from materials like merino wool or high-performance synthetics. These fabrics regulate your body temperature and wick moisture away from your skin, ensuring you stay comfortably dry.

Mid Layer: Include insulating mid layers, such as fleece jackets or down vests, in your mountain capsule. These pieces provide much-needed warmth and can be easily added or removed as the temperature fluctuates.

Outer Layer: Equip yourself with a waterproof and windproof jacket that can shield you from rain, snow, and the chilling mountain winds. Seek out a jacket with breathable features to prevent overheating during strenuous activities.

Don't neglect your lower half, either. Insulated trousers or leggings can be a lifesaver in colder mountain climates. You can wear them alone or layered under waterproof trousers, providing extra protection against the cold. For socks, opt for moisture-wicking options constructed from wool or synthetic materials to keep your feet dry and blister-free. If icy conditions are expected, consider adding thermal or long underwear to your base layer for additional warmth.

And don't forget accessories! A warm hat that covers your ears, a cosy scarf, and insulated gloves are essential for safeguarding your extremities from the biting cold. For convenience, look for touch-screen-compatible gloves, allowing you to use your phone without exposing your hands to the elements.

The Three C's

Adequate footwear is critical. Whether you choose boots or hiking shoes, ensure they offer proper insulation and traction. Remember to break them in before your trip to avoid painful blisters that could derail your mountain holiday.

Lastly, remember to bring a selection of cosy and comfortable outfits for unwinding in the evenings after a day of mountain trekking. Include comfy loungewear, flannel pyjamas, and warm socks. A well-planned mountain capsule guarantees that you're equipped to fully savour the splendour of Mother Nature, relish cosy evenings with your loved ones, and surmount any challenges the mountains may present you.

Desert Safari

When gearing up for a desert adventure, your choice of clothing can make all the difference in ensuring comfort under the scorching sun during the day and keeping you warm during the chilly desert nights.

Select garments that offer protection from the intense heat and relentless sun. Look for lightweight, loose-fitting, and breathable attire that facilitates air circulation and helps you stay cool in the desert's unforgiving climate. Cotton and linen fabrics are your best allies in these arid landscapes.

While it might be tempting to pack short-sleeved T-shirts and shorts, long-sleeved shirts and trousers are the wiser choice. They shield your skin from the harsh sun rays to provide a barrier against sunburn. Opt for light-coloured clothing, which reflects the sun's heat. For example, desert nomads often draped themselves in long robes made from light colours.

While the desert may be synonymous with searing daytime sun, the nights can bring a significant drop in temperature. Include a lightweight jacket, sweater, or shawl for when the desert chill sets in.

Invest in a wide-brimmed hat or a cap to safeguard yourself from the sun's relentless rays. Look for headwear made with natural fibres or with built-in ventilation to keep your head cool. Remember to pack sunglasses with UV protection to shield your eyes from the intense desert sunlight. Opt for sunglasses that offer ample coverage and are polarized to reduce glare. Bring a lightweight scarf or bandana that can be draped over your face and neck during sandstorms.

Prioritize comfortable, sturdy, closed-toe shoes or desert boots that provide protection against the searing hot sand, sharp rocks, and the potential threat of snake bites. Steer clear of open-toe shoes, sandals, or trainers, as they are ill-suited for desert exploration. I learned this lesson the hard way during my first desert safari in Dubai. My mesh Nike trainers filled with sand, which I could never completely remove.

Lastly, if your desert itinerary includes visits to oases, springs, or wadis, remember to pack your swimwear for a refreshing dip in these natural desert gems.

With the proper clothing and gear, you can fully immerse yourself in the unique beauty and challenges of the desert, allowing you to make the most of your desert adventure.

Jungle Trek

When embarking on a jungle expedition, your choice of clothing can make or break your comfort in this lush and challenging environment. Moisture-wicking clothes, protective long sleeves, and cargo pants are your best allies.

Prioritize garments crafted from lightweight and breathable fabrics like cotton or moisture-wicking synthetic blends. These materials are your secret weapon against the jungle's oppressive humidity, ensuring you remain fresh and comfortable throughout your adventure. Long sleeves and trousers serve multiple purposes: defence against insects, sunburn, and the inevitable scratches from thick vegetation. During my trip to the Amazon rainforest, I was immensely grateful for packing long, breathable cargo pants. They shielded my legs from the relentless mosquitoes, ensuring I could appreciate the jungle's beauty and engage with indigenous communities without the constant worry of itching, scratching, or the threat of malaria.

Pack a reliable waterproof raincoat or poncho against the frequent and unpredictable jungle rain showers. This essential gear will keep you dry when the heavens open unexpectedly. Additionally, consider investing in a waterproof bag or dry sack to safeguard your belongings from moisture.

Choose sturdy, comfortable hiking boots or trail shoes with excellent traction. Look for options that offer breathability to prevent your feet from becoming uncomfortably sweaty. Ankle support is crucial, as the uneven jungle terrain can pose challenges. Pack a pair of lightweight, quick-drying sandals to navigate river crossings or simply unwind at camp. These versatile companions are perfect for keeping your feet fresh and comfortable in wet conditions.

Lastly, don't forget to include a swimsuit in your jungle gear. Whether you plan to visit rivers, waterfalls, or serene jungle pools, a swimsuit allows you to take a refreshing dip and connect with

Mother Nature. With the right clothing and gear, your jungle adventure can be a memorable and enjoyable experience, connecting you with the vibrant ecosystems of this captivating environment.

Sailing Trip

Preparing for a sailing adventure, especially during events like Yacht Week, requires careful consideration of the ever-changing conditions on the water. While it promises fabulous experiences, the sea can quickly turn challenging if you're not adequately equipped. Expect the journey to bring hot days, crisp nights, and potentially uncomfortable situations when the winds pick up.

Prioritize lightweight and breathable fabrics that dry swiftly. This may be cotton or merino wool, depending on where you sail and the prevailing temperatures. Although cotton doesn't retain heat when wet, cotton is an excellent choice for summer T-shirts and long-sleeve shirts as it's fresh and breathable on hot sunny days. Merino wool is excellent as a base layer in colder climates, as it's soft and comfy and doesn't hold onto odour or moisture. Alternatively, look for garments from moisture-wicking synthetic blends for your base layer. Pack a selection of shorts to keep you comfortable on warm days and remember to include lightweight trousers or capris for fresh evenings and sun protection. Also, bring one or two sweaters or cardigans on hand for chilly evenings or unexpected drops in temperature. Plus, you can always drape the cardigan casually over your shoulders for that timeless, "old money" look.

Depending on the specific conditions, it's wise to take waterproof clothing to keep you dry in case of rain or splashing waves. While a wind and waterproof jacket may suffice for occasional

The Three C's

summer outings, serious sailors know the value of proper sailing gear. I vividly remember sailing off the coast of Barcelona when my glee waned as the weather took a bad turn. The wind picked up, and thick clouds obscured the sun, leaving me uncomfortably cold and reaching for my husband's jacket. Investing in a high-quality sailing kit is advisable if you plan to spend considerable time on the water, especially in challenging weather conditions. This includes waterproof jacket and trousers, as well as items like gloves and a life jacket.

Don't leave the dock without a hat that can withstand the gusty winds. Caps are the optimal choice. While wide-brimmed hats are fabulous, they run the risk of being swept away. In the best-case scenario, your captain will promptly change course to retrieve it. In the worst-case scenario, it will find its resting place on the ocean floor. Avoid this by bringing a hat which can be secured on your head. High-quality sunglasses, and a trusty supply of sunscreen to shield your skin from the sun's unrelenting rays are also must-haves. If your sailing adventure involves a lot of water sports, consider packing UV-protective clothing or rash guards to keep you comfortable and protected.

Invest in a good pair of sailing shoes that can serve a dual purpose, both on deck and ashore. Unlike some trainers that can leave unsightly marks on the yacht's deck, sailing shoes are designed to provide traction without causing damage. This way, you can comfortably move around the boat without worrying about leaving unwanted marks.

Swimsuits are a must for any sailing trip. I always recommend bringing several pairs. Having multiple options ensures you always have a dry suit to slip into, even after a dip in the sea. I typically rotate between two or three throughout the day to stay comfortable. Include one or two sarongs or cover-ups to pair with your swimwear. Finally, it's a smart move to invest in a waterproof dry bag. This invaluable accessory will keep your valuables, electronics, and extra clothing safe and dry.

With the proper clothing and gear, your yacht trip will be a smooth sailing. You can fully appreciate the beauty of the being out at sea while staying comfortable and prepared for whatever challenges the ocean might toss your way.

Tropical Destinations

Travelling to exotic tropical locales such as Indonesia, Thailand, Kenya, Nigeria, Colombia, India, Mexico, or Brazil promises a thrilling adventure. However, it also calls for smart packing choices to ensure comfort in hot and humid weather.

Prioritize lightweight and breathable fabrics. Loose-fitting attire crafted from cotton, rayon, viscose, or linen will be your best companions in these climates. These materials allow the gentle breeze to circulate your body, ensuring you remain cool and at ease, even when the tropical sun is at its peak. An intimate detail worth noting: in tropical high humidity, undergarments made from natural fabrics, such as cotton, are your best bet for staying comfortable. Exercise caution when considering local laundries for delicate clothing items, as they may not handle them with the necessary care. I've learned this the hard way. I had many silk tops and dainty underwear ruined by laundry services in Bali and Mozambique.

The ultraviolet index is high in tropical destinations. Sun protection is non-negotiable. Pack hats, sunglasses with UV

The Three C's

protection, and an ample supply of sunscreen. Also, include light-weight, long-sleeved shirts or cover-ups that provide an extra layer of defence against sunburn. These versatile items can also come to your rescue in air-conditioned indoor spaces, where the temperature can feel quite chilly. To stay comfortable in these frigid environments, you can also bring a light sweater or shawl to easily slip on and off.

Your choice of footwear should balance comfort and practicality. Comfortable sandals, flip-flops, and lightweight, breathable closed shoes are essential. These options allow your feet to breathe while providing support for your explorations. In tropical regions, sudden rain showers are common. Opt for footwear that won't be easily ruined by water and dirt. Leather designer sneakers may not be the best choice for these destinations. Instead, consider mesh trainers or foam sandals. And, of course, never set out without a pair of flip-flops or water shoes, a must for beach activities and impromptu dips in the ocean.

Comfort

Embarking on a trip is all about experiencing the world, soaking in breath-taking sights, immersing in art, connecting with nature, relishing the atmosphere of bustling town squares, engaging in serendipitous encounters with locals, savouring delectable cuisine, and indulging in retail therapy. In all of this, one thing is most important: your comfort.

Your clothing choices should not only make you look good but also make you feel at ease. When planning your travel capsule, avoid items that don't suit you, whether they pinch in the wrong places, hinder your movement, or lead to profuse sweating. Uncomfortable attire can dampen your enjoyment and remain untouched in your suitcase. Unlike your home closet, where items may collect dust unnoticed, each piece in your travel luggage must earn its place. Weight limits are at stake and every item should contribute to a comfortable and enjoyable trip.

I am a planner, particularly on short trips where I aim to make the most of every hour of the holiday. I prefer having a list of our planned activities, locations, transportation options, weather forecasts, and any relevant cultural factors. However, if you're more of a happy-go-lucky traveller, you don't need a detailed itinerary for every activity. A general idea should suffice.

Begin by considering the activities you'll be indulging in during your journey. If your plans include exploring a city, visiting museums, leisurely strolls along boulevards, shopping excursions, and idyllic coffee breaks in charming cafes, your clothing and accessories should embody a harmonious blend of comfort and style.

- **Comfortable Shoes:** Given the likelihood of extensive walking, a pair of comfortable shoes is non-negotiable. Sneakers or well-cushioned flat shoes are your trusted allies.
- **Layering:** Incorporate versatile layering pieces, like a light blazer or sweater, to adapt seamlessly to fluctuating temperatures.
- **Practical Bag:** Don't forget a chic yet functional backpack, cross-body bag, or tote to carry your daily essentials.

For those planning an active holiday replete with hiking adventures, long drives, and visits to archaeological wonders, prioritizing comfort and functionality in your clothing choices is paramount.

- **Sturdy Footwear:** Include supportive hiking boots or trail shoes for comfortable exploration.
- **Athletic Attire:** Pack lightweight, moisture-wicking athletic outfits suitable for physically demanding activities.
- **Layering Essentials**: Ensure you have adaptable pieces, such as a fleece jacket or vest, a hoodie, a sweater, and a jacket to counter varying weather conditions.
- **Carry-All:** A handy backpack is essential to accommodate essentials and hydration during your activities.

Alternatively, relaxation and comfort are key if your agenda revolves around unwinding on sun-kissed beaches and making occasional gym and spa visits.

- **Swimwear:** Pack multiple swimsuits for lounging by the beach and swimming.
- **Chic Cover-Ups:** Lightweight cover-ups, like dresses, sarongs, and co-ords, offer an effortless transition from water to land.
- **Athletic Gear:** Carry moisture-wicking athletic wear for gym sessions or sport activities.
- **Footwear Choices:** Opt for comfortable, supportive shoes for workouts and chic sandals or slides for navigating the hotel grounds.
- **Beach Tote:** A spacious beach bag is indispensable for carrying your essentials.

Beyond activities, contemplate your accommodation and the time you'll spend there. Hotels usually provide slippers and bathrobes for guests, but if you're staying at an Airbnb or a friend's place, consider packing loungewear and house shoes. Slipping into fresh clothes and soft slippers after a day of sightseeing will help you feel more and home and help you wind down.

Culture

Planning your travel capsule requires a careful consideration of the cultural norms at your destination. Beyond showing respect for the local customs, it enriches your travel experience.

In the heart of destinations such as Saudi Arabia or Iran, modest dressing is not just appreciated but expected. In India, modest attire is also favoured, emphasizing clothing that conceals your arms and legs. Other countries that prefer modesty include some in Southeast Asia such as Thailand, Indonesia, and Vietnam, and extends to countries like China and Japan, where a modest dress code is expected at temples or religious settings.

Lightweight, loose clothing is a common choice for travellers in these destinations, offering comfort in the warm climate while adhering to cultural norms. A scarf or shawl can be a handy accessory, doubling up as an extra layer or a head cover when required.

The conversation around traditional Islamic garments like abayas and burqas is varied and complex. While some view them as symbols of oppression, others see laws banning these garments as an infringement on religious freedom. Regardless of the perspective, when you're in a country where such attire is standard, respecting the dress code is crucial.

Some exceptions exist in cosmopolitan cities like Dubai and Bangkok, which have a more relaxed approach to attire due to their diverse populations. Still, the fundamental principle of dressing modestly and respectfully remains, especially when visiting cultural and religious sites. For instance, once I was denied entry to the Mohammed Bin Rashid Library in Dubai due to wearing a skirt above the knee. That experience taught me a valuable lesson. Now, when visiting museums or cultural landmarks in the UAE, I wear long dresses or loose-fitting, full-length trousers.

It's always a good practice to research your destination's customs and traditions. Dressing appropriately can foster connections with locals, enhancing your travel experience. Being respectful and aware of the local standards not only showcases you as a considerate traveller but also opens doors to more authentic cultural experiences.

Integrating traditional clothing or accessories can reflect your appreciation for the local culture. However, be careful to avoid cultural misappropriation. Cultural appropriation is when elements from one culture are used by individuals or groups from another culture, often without proper understanding or respect for their significance. For instance, African and Asian traditional clothing often carry a significant cultural meaning. Wearing these without understanding their context can be offensive.

In African nations, traditional attire like the Maasai clothing or Kente cloth is not just fabric but a symbol of rituals, status, and heritage. In Asia, a garment like the Japanese kimono isn't just attire but a bearer of a rich historical narrative. Approach these items respectfully, seek guidance from locals on their proper wear, and support local artisans through your purchases.

Taking cultural, comfort, and climate considerations into account, your travel capsule should be a blend of style and sensibility. By keeping these elements in mind, you'll be equipped for every adventure and cultural encounter that comes your way, enhancing not just your travel album but your global perspective.

The Three C's

Chapter 2

The Base of Your Travel Capsule

I n a world where every item in your suitcase must earn its place to avoid breaching the weight limit, you must master the art of efficient packing. No more squeezing in that whimsical skirt that, let's be honest, might never see the light of day. Instead, the savvy traveller embraces the concept of a travel capsule — a selection that's thoughtfully curated for versatility, capable of seamlessly adapting to shifting weather, activities, and even personal inclinations. But how do you master this skill?

When constructing your travel capsule, each item you pack should be a multitasking hero, contributing to several outfits. The goal is to maximize the utility of your clothing and accessories.

To achieve this, the spotlight shines on basic pieces, which should constitute approximately seventy percent of your travel ensemble. The essence of a solid base is to possess a collection of fundamental garments that seamlessly meld with one another, forming a versatile foundation for diverse looks, all without overburdening your luggage. Ideally, one piece should dovetail seamlessly into at least three distinct looks.

Decoding the Base

So, what is a base wardrobe? The first time I grasped this concept during a styling masterclass was a revelation. It felt as if the heavens had opened, and I finally gained clarity about why my wardrobe was bursting with clothes that I struggled to combine into outfits.

A base wardrobe is an ensemble of elegantly simple, neutral-hued pieces free of intricate cuts, lavish embellishments, or overpowering prints. The beauty lies in their chameleon-like quality, allowing them to adapt and harmonize. Classic pieces such as muted blouses, versatile bottoms, foundational dresses, and quintessential footwear choices like pristine white trainers, basic sandals, versatile boots, or classic pumps are all part of your base. While a good base is important for a functional day-to-day wardrobe, it is the foundation of your travel capsule.

When constructing your base for your travel capsule, a pragmatic approach involves zeroing in on two or three harmonious colours to form the backbone of your attire. For instance, if you harbour an affinity for a particular hue like serene blue or lush green, let it guide your base selections. However, if your wardrobe predominantly whispers in tones of beige, taupe, grey, or classic black, embrace these neutrals. Their timelessness and flexibility make them perfect for conjuring both minimalist and sophisticated looks. In the subsequent chapters of this book, I'll offer curated colour recommendations tailored to each destination, so you do not always have to make these choices yourself.

Base Vs. Statement Pieces

As you craft your travel capsule, it's crucial to differentiate between base items and statement pieces. There are always tell-tale signs. Here are a few examples of elements that mean it is not a base item:

- **Embellishments:** Base items are typically free from excessive embellishments like beading, sequins, or lace. These decorations often categorize an item as a statement piece, making it more formal, dressy, and less versatile than plain, neutral items.
- **Bold Prints and Patterns:** Base items tend to feature solid colours or subtle patterns. Bold, eye-catching prints are usually reserved for statement pieces. They're the firecrackers, adding a burst of visual intrigue to your look.
- **Ruffle and Frills:** Base items embrace simplicity, making them less likely to have many ruffles or frills. While these details can add a cute, romantic touch, they limit an item's versatility compared to plainer items.
- **Logos and Branding:** Base items typically avoid excessive branding or logos, as these can make them harder to pair with other pieces. Also, logomania might be overwhelming or inappropriate in many destinations.

The Basics

While base items form the core of your travel capsule, statement pieces have their special place. These bold and eye-catching items can add a touch of personal style, make a trendy fashion statement, and inject excitement into your outfits. In addition, they provide an opportunity for self-expression and can be a fun way to elevate your look when mixed and matched with your base items. Whether it's a vibrantly patterned blouse, a unique accessory, or a trendy jacket, these statement pieces instantly transform a simple outfit into something special.

However, it's essential to strike a balance and prevent statement pieces from overpowering your entire capsule. A general guideline is to limit statement pieces to around 30% of your overall selection. This ensures that they complement your base items instead of dominating them.

Consider the versatility of a piece even when you are integrating statement pieces. Look for items that can be mixed and matched with different tops, bottoms, and accessories, allowing you to create multiple looks. This approach maximizes the impact of statement pieces while maintaining a cohesive and practical travel capsule.

As your travel capsule takes shape, view base and statement pieces as instrumentalists in an orchestra. Base items are the steady rhythm section, grounding the melody with consistency and adaptability. Statement pieces are the soloists stepping in at moments to elevate the tune with distinct notes.

By adhering to this balanced composition, you're not just packing a bag. You're orchestrating a travel capsule that's ready to echo your style narrative across diverse settings, each outfit a verse in your travel story, harmonious yet distinctly individual.

The Basics

Using Colour in Your Travel Capsule

The use of colour can be a captivating art form. It can breathe life into your attire, infusing it with character and even reflecting the ambiance of your chosen destination. Let's look at various colour combinations that can serve as your muse for constructing a striking travel capsule.

Red, Yellow, and Blue: This trio forms the classic primary colour scheme, injecting your outfits with a bold and vivacious essence, ideal for urban adventures during the vibrant seasons of spring and summer. The dynamic interplay between red, yellow, and blue fosters an atmosphere of energy and liveliness. To strike a harmonious balance, complement these primary hues with the timeless elegance of white and black.

Green, Purple, Orange: Picture a palette that takes its cues from the natural world, perfect for outdoor pursuits like hiking, camping, or serene retreats. The combination of green, purple, and orange mirrors the equilibrium in the great outdoors, blending warm and cool tones harmoniously. This particular colour combo shines brightest in tropical and exotic settings, where nature's beauty dances in vibrant hues. Complement these shades with earthy neutrals like beige, brown, and black.

Pink, Purple, Yellow: For those seeking a whimsical and feminine touch, this trifecta of pastel charm creates an aura of playfulness and grace, well-suited to the enchanting backdrop of romantic

European destinations. The soft and delightful blend of pink, purple, and yellow can transport you into a world of charm and whimsy. Enhance this effect by mingling these shades with the freshness of white and beige.

Brown, Yellow, and Blue: Venture into the realm of rustic elegance, a natural triad that harmonizes beautifully with countryside exploration and leisurely escapes. The earthy, inviting tones of brown, yellow, and blue echo the serene atmosphere of rural landscapes. Allow these warm hues to entwine with the simplicity of greys and whites for a truly serene effect.

Black and White: The timeless duo of black and white knows no bounds. It emerges as a versatile choice capable of crafting bold and contemporary looks, perfectly adaptable to a variety of urban settings. The striking contrast between these two monochromatic pillars allows you to embrace a minimalist aesthetic while exuding sophistication.

In addition to these combinations, neutral tones stand as a dependable and timeless option for your travel capsule base. By blending the soothing shades of beige, taupe, grey, and white, you create a canvas that adapts effortlessly to any destination or occasion. When in doubt, neutrals always offer a safe and stylish choice.

When working with colour, consider some fundamental principles of colour theory. Avoid clashing with bright and dull shades, such contrasts can disrupt the harmony of your look. Stick to colours within the same family or opt for colours opposite to each other or adjacent on the colour wheel to create a cohesive appearance.

Colour wheel apps can be invaluable tools for those who need clarification on which colours complement each other.

Using Colour

Experimenting with different combinations using colour wheel apps can help you craft outfits that convey your desired impression.

Remember that your choice of colours significantly influences your outfits' aesthetics and mood. By thoughtfully selecting and coordinating your colour palette, you can construct a harmonious travel capsule that reflects your personality and lets you capture the perfect travel photos.

Using Colour

Chapter 3

Accessorize to Mesmerize

Accessories are the secret weapon in your travel capsule, capable of transforming your outfits from nice to wow! As you trot the globe, these tiny essentials accentuate your outfits and add variety to your looks. Let's dive into accessories, including how to choose and pick shoes, handbags, hats, sunglasses, and jewellery for your journey. To simplify the process, I recommend you finalize your clothing choices before selecting accessories. Once you've determined your clothing's colours and textures, picking the perfect accessories becomes a breeze.

Like clothing, choose accessories based on your destination, expected weather, and planned activities. If hiking trails and windy cliff-top walks are in the itinerary, those dazzling stilettos, no matter how recently purchased or how ardent their appeal, might need to sit this one out. Contrarily, if your vacation has slots reserved for chic restaurants or a posh event, those shoes can be your statement piece.

Luggage weight restrictions are the Achilles' heel of every fashion-forward traveller. While shoes and handbags are essential, they can be the heavyweights tipping the scales in the wrong direction. Minimizing the number of shoes and handbags you pack is essential. The strategy is to choose one or two versatile items that can complement multiple outfits.

Handbags

I have a weakness for handbags. Throughout the years, I've curated a collection that includes vintage, designer, and high-street pieces. And I adore each one. When it comes to travelling, the temptation to bring a handbag for every outfit can be strong, so I often face some difficult decisions. I recommend bringing one or two daytime bags and one evening bag, each serving its unique purpose. For your daytime bag, versatility and practicality should be your primary considerations. Look for a bag that can double as a travel bag, accommodating essentials like a water bottle, your phone, documents, makeup, or an umbrella. Include a backpack or beach bag if your itinerary involves outdoor activities or beach outings. Due to its large size, this can be your carry-on during the flight.

Balancing practicality and style is the key to accessorizing for your trip. To make the best choices, consider your destination, expected weather conditions, and planned activities. In Part II of this book, I'll provide specific bag recommendations tailored to different

Accessories

destinations. For now, let's explore some general daytime bag suggestions based on travel themes.

City Breaks: Opt for a smart yet functional cross-body bag or a medium-sized tote that can hold your essentials while you explore urban landscapes. A leather backpack can also be a great choice depending on your style.

Countryside Adventures: Choose a spacious leather backpack or a canvas shoulder bag that embodies rustic-chic aesthetics while allowing you to carry necessities for your countryside excursions.

Mountain Escapes: Prioritize durability with a backpack or waterproof messenger bag to accommodate hiking essentials.

Island Getaways: Embrace tropical vibes with a lightweight woven tote or a straw beach bag, offering ample space for your beach essentials.

Safari Expeditions: Opt for a sturdy and compact safari-style, cross-body bag or a functional backpack that keeps your belongings secure and easily accessible during wildlife adventures.

Tropical Destinations: Consider a vibrant shoulder bag or a small cross-body bag crafted from lightweight, water-resistant materials.

When the sun dips and the city lights glitter, your evening bag becomes the spotlight. When it comes to evening bags, clutches, and small shoulder bags are ideal choices. They exude elegance and occupy minimal space in your suitcase. Select materials like satin,

Accessories

velvet, or leather in classic colours such as black or metallic tones for versatility and timeless style.

The bag's material, size, and weight should align with your destination and activities. For instance, Nappa leather may not fare well in wet climates, making canvas or straw bags more suitable. If your trip involves extensive sightseeing, opt for a lightweight and compact bag to ease your daily excursions.

Lastly, consider safety. If you're heading to a destination notorious for pickpocketing, choose a cross-body or belt bag to enhance security and comfort amid bustling streets.

Shoes

Just like clothing and handbags, choosing the appropriate footwear is paramount for a seamless travel experience. Key factors to consider when it comes to choosing your footwear are the surface of the streets, how much walking you plan to do, and how you plan to get around. All these factors should inform your selection of shoes. Ill-fitting or inappropriate footwear can quickly turn your dream vacation into a nightmare scenario.

For a visit to Rome, a city known for its magnificent historic sites, romantic fountains, and cobblestone streets, comfortable and sturdy shoes are a must. Opt for flat shoes like sandals, espadrilles, loafers, or sneakers that provide support and cushioning for walking long distances. And avoid high heels for daytime activities! I recall travelling to Prague in my early twenties (another European capital with its cobblestone streets) and making the mistake of packing a pair of stiletto booties! I felt pretty foolish as I hobbled along the

Accessories

uneven surfaces, casting envious glances at another lady who looked both comfortable and stylish in her white sneakers.

For a trip to Marrakech, prioritize breathable and comfortable footwear like closed-toe sandals, espadrilles, or mules, allowing your feet to stay fresh in the heat. These options work well for exploring the city and its historical sites. Steer clear of high heels, which are impractical on uneven pavements.

In Paris, a city made for wandering and exploring on foot, it's important to have comfortable and sturdy shoes. Opt for ballet flats, ankle boots, or loafers depending on the weather. A low heel or the classic white sneaker also provides comfort and style while walking around the city and visiting famous sites and museums.

For a trip to Bali, a tropical destination with stunning beaches and plenty of outdoor activities, prioritise sturdy sandals, slides, and flip-flops. Pack a pair of light mesh trainers for exploring the great outdoors, climbing volcanoes, or riding scooters through crazy traffic. Pick shoes with adequate grip. Avoid shoes made from delicate leather and suede, which are unsuitable for wet and sandy conditions.

Evening shoes are an opportunity to add a touch of elegance to your outfit. Whether planning outfits for dinners, a night out on the town, or a special event, a beautiful pair of shoes can elevate your look. Opt for heels or dressy sandals that complement several evening outfits. A pair of sleek stilettos can add sophistication and edge to a cocktail dress or tailored pantsuit. Alternatively, strappy sandals with embellishments or metallic accents can bring a touch of glamour to a little black dress or a chic jumpsuit. Look for shoes with cushioned insoles or low-block heels that offer stability without sacrificing style. By selecting the perfect pair of evening shoes, you'll feel confident and ready to make a stylish statement wherever the night takes you.

Accessories

Adorn with Caution: Travel Jewellery

When it comes to jewellery during your travels, adopting a "less is more" approach is both prudent and sometimes culturally sensitive. First of all, flashy and expensive jewellery can unwittingly make you a target for pickpockets and potential crimes. Prioritizing your safety means avoiding unnecessary attention that could lead to theft or harm. When you travel, it's best to err on the side of caution.

Furthermore, in many developing countries, a significant portion of the population lives in poverty. Flaunting excessive wealth through extravagant jewellery can be disrespectful and offensive. When travelling to developing countries, minimal jewellery is the wisest choice.

That said, there are destinations where wearing statement pieces can be completely safe and culturally appropriate. These countries typically have low crime rates and stable political climates, making them more conducive to displaying bold jewellery. Here are a few examples:

United Arab Emirates (UAE): The UAE is known for its low crime rate and is globally considered one of the safest countries. With luxury shopping and high-end fashion, it's a place where statement jewellery fits right in.

Japan: Japan boasts safety and a low crime rate. Japanese people take pride in their appearance, and dressing up is a common practice. As a result, wearing statement jewellery can blend seamlessly with local culture.

Accessories

Oman and Qatar: These Middle Eastern nations are known for their safety and stability. The local population appreciates fashion and elegance.

Singapore: Singapore is another safe destination with low crime rates. People often dress well and take pride in their appearance, so wearing bold jewellery aligns with the local scene.

Iceland and Switzerland: Known for their wealth and affluence, people tend to be well-dressed. Statement jewellery wouldn't seem out of place here. These countries are considered safe havens with low crime rates.

Regardless of your destination's safety, it's essential to exercise caution and situational awareness. Consider factors such as where you will be staying, how you will get around, and what activities you plan to do. Research local customs and cultural norms regarding jewellery to avoid any faux pas. For example, the French openly disdain ostentatious displays of wealth, especially by young women. Stay informed about recent crime statistics and security changes when planning your trip.

Scarves, Hats, & Sunglasses

Scarves, hats, and sunglasses are not only practical because they shield you from the elements but also offer an excellent opportunity to express your individuality and fashion sensibilities during your travels. When packing hats, take care to preserve their shape. Wear them on the flight or place them in the overhead compartment above your hand luggage to prevent damage.

Hats

When it comes to sunny destinations, a wide-brimmed hat is your best companion to protect your face and neck from the sun's rays. If you're aiming for a more casual style, a cap is a great choice. On the other hand, when heading to colder destinations, make sure to pack a cosy beanie, a warm cap, a beret, or a woollen fedora. Your hat should harmonize with your style and match the colours of your travel capsule. Choose a neutral colour that can easily complement various looks.

Consider investing in a high-quality piece that can stand the test of time. I remember a vacation in the South of France when I stepped into this lovely hat shop, and there it was: a beautiful white Panama hat with a broad, black ribbon that stole my heart. It's a classic piece that pairs effortlessly with almost any outfit. It's been a part of my collection for four years now, looking just as exquisite as the day I got it.

Accessories

Scarves

Scarves not only provide warmth and comfort but also inject a pop of colour and style into your outfits. Look for large pashminas that can double as a scarf, headcover, or even a light throw during your flight. Choose scarves with patterns and colours that harmonize with multiple pieces in your travel capsule so you can create diverse looks with minimal items.

One of my all-time favourites is the exquisite Hermes Carré scarf. This versatile accessory exudes timeless elegance and offers endless styling possibilities. You can wear it in the classic neck-wrap style or get creative by using it as a headband, a statement belt, or a chic halter top (perfect for sunny destinations). It can be layered under a winter jacket in colder climates, peeking out to reveal its intricate design. You don't need to break the bank to get one of these. Many vintage stores and online platforms sell pre-loved Hermes scarves in excellent condition. I found mine on Vestiaire Collective. However, consider the weather and safety aspects before packing such a valuable item for your trip.

Sunglasses

Sunglasses protect your eyes from harmful UV rays and add style to your appearance. Personally, I enjoy experimenting with different sunglass styles and have built quite a collection over the years. However, when it comes to travel, I find choosing one pair that complements all my outfits is wise. Typically, I opt for a classic pair with full-black lenses, a black frame, and minimal embellishments.

When selecting sunglasses, prioritise UV protection, especially in hot and sunny destinations. Choose sunglasses that align with your style, whether classy, sporty, or funky. Remember to pack a soft protective case to keep your sunglasses safe during your travels. Lastly, be mindful that sea salt and moisture can affect metallic trims and screws on sunglasses, so always remember to rinse them off and properly dry them after a beach outing.

While embracing the styling opportunities these accessories provide, always bear in mind the golden rule of accessories: "Less stuff means more freedom." After all, isn't freedom one of the true joys of travel?

Chapter 4

Unleash Your Inner Stylist

*N*ow that you've meticulously reviewed your wardrobe and have a clear idea of the essential items, statement pieces, and accessories you'd like to take on your trip, it's time to unleash your inner stylist. By experimenting with combinations, you'll discover what works well and what doesn't. It might seem daunting. But trust me, it's a lot of fun! Investing this time now will save you countless frustrated mornings when you're faced with the feeling of having nothing to wear during your trip (not to mention the burden of packing items you'll never actually use). Set aside one or two hours, put on your favourite tunes, and ensure your phone is charged and ready to capture photos of your outfit choices. Think of it as your very own movie montage!

Putting It All Together

Begin by gathering all the clothes and accessories you intend to take and placing them on flat surfaces like the floor or bed. Next, categorize your items by type, separating tops, bottoms, and dresses, creating distinct piles for each. Ensure that each item is visible, so you can have an overview of your selection and see potential outfit combinations.

With your items sorted into distinct piles, you can begin experimenting with various pairings to create unique looks. For instance, try pairing each top with different bottoms to gauge how well they complement each other. Alternatively, take a dress and explore how it can be styled with various jumpers and jackets. This process serves as a quick and easy way to generate outfit ideas. Aim to create at least three different looks with each item. If you notice an item doesn't pair well with more than one or two others, consider leaving it behind. Granted, some statement pieces can be very unique and challenging to style with other items. In this case, ensure they comprise less than 30% of the clothes you plan to take. When you find an item that isn't working as hard as it should, put it into a "maybe" pile.

Next, try the outfits on and assess how they fit. While this may appear overkill to some, trust me, it's an essential part of the process. You need to know that your outfits not only look good but also feel good. Far too often, we pack outfits only to discover during our trip they don't fit properly. Once, a friend visited me in Dubai for New Year's celebrations and packed a dress for the big night out

Assembling

without trying it on beforehand. When it came time to prepare for the countdown, she realized the dress wouldn't zip up because she gained some weight since the last time she wore it.

As you try on each look, move around and pay attention to how it feels. Assess the comfort level, how the fabric drapes, and whether it flatters your body. This is especially critical for any archive pieces or items you purchased online. Sometimes, an item may look fantastic on a hanger or a model, but not the human who wants to wear it. It's essential to give yourself the opportunity to assess how the clothing suits your current body shape. Our bodies change over time, from month to month and even from day to day. Therefore, it's crucial that the clothes you select work well with your present physique. Equally significant is how the outfit makes you feel. Choose outfits that instil confidence and a sense of feeling good about yourself.

Additionally, trying on different outfits before your journey enables you to identify any fit, comfort, or style issues that may require attention—perhaps a loose button here or some minor adjustments there. Such issues are common, and it's better to address them while you're still at home. Moreover, it provides clarity and peace of mind, ensuring that your outfits make you feel fantastic and fully prepared to conquer the world.

I like to do this three or four days before my trip. Typically, I set aside an evening during the week or an afternoon on the weekend to go through the whole process. I won't lie, I have so much fun with it. It takes me back to my teenage years when I'd spend hours experimenting with various outfits in front of the mirror. Doing it well before my flight gives me ample time to make alterations or buy missing items. Approach this stage with a sense of enjoyment and creativity. After all, clothing serves as a medium for expressing your unique style and character.

Assembling

Creating a Visual Reference

While trying different looks, I advise you to snap a photo of the ones you like. Taking pictures of the combinations you create serves two functions. First, it provides a quick insight into which items are versatile and create many outfits. Then you can identify the items that are unquestionably worth including in your packing list and those that warrant re-evaluation. Secondly, these photos serve as a convenient reference when you're accessorizing. Finally, these pictures will serve as a lookbook and facilitate your outfit selection during your trip.

As you flip through the photos, pay attention to the pieces that you featured in multiple outfits. These are the true workhorses of your capsule and should be considered must-haves for your trip. On the other hand, items that feature in just one or two outfits may not be suitable choices for this specific trip. Set them aside for future occasions.

Furthermore, outfit photos offer a glimpse into the accessory and jewellery options that can complement and complete your looks. Reviewing the pictures lets you swiftly determine what accessories you should bring to enhance and complete your ensembles.

Also, having a visual reference of your final outfit choices will streamline the packing process and alleviate stress, allowing you to focus on other aspects of your trip preparation.

Finally, beyond being an invaluable aid during the preparation stage, an album of your selected looks on your phone will be a tremendous time-saver during your trip. I like to create a dedicated photo album on my phone featuring my final outfit choices. This visual reference eliminates the need to ponder what to wear each morning. It proves especially helpful when you're battling jet lag and must get ready quickly. Every morning of my trip, I simply scroll through the album, select an outfit I'm feeling that day, and I'm dressed within five minutes!

Ultimately, this approach will save you a significant amount of time and reduce dressing-related stress during your trip. As a result, you'll spend less time worrying about what to wear, avoid wearing the same pair of jeans every day, and have more time to enjoy your vacation!

Pre-Trip Shopping

During the process of assembling looks, you will probably find that you're missing one or two items. I encourage mindful shopping, making a list of all the items you're missing, from clothing and shoes to accessories and other essentials. Having a list keeps you focused and streamlines the shopping process, making it faster, easier, and more cost-effective.

Also, bear in mind the items you purchase for your trip should have long-term use beyond the vacation. While it can be tempting to indulge in a whole new wardrobe for your trip, this approach is neither sustainable nor good for your bank account. Avoid buying items that you are unlikely to wear again. They will only take up space in your closet afterward. When considering purchasing an item, ask yourself: "Can I integrate this item into looks in my daily life? Where can I wear this to? Does this work with the rest of my wardrobe?"

Of course, sometimes there are items we want to get for our trip, but we struggle to integrate them into our daily lives. For example, if you're living in New York and want to buy a chic cover-up

Assembling

for your getaway in Fiji, it's unlikely you'll need it back in the city. Or you live in a tropical climate, and you're looking for a jacket for your magical European Christmas break. In this case, invest in one classic piece that will stand the test of time. You can neatly store it away and find it for your next vacation in the region. Avoid buying items that follow the latest trends or have too many embellishments or loud prints and logos.

I make an annual journey to Bali to visit my father. My Bali capsule includes items from my everyday wardrobe in Dubai, such as simple tops, a wrap skirt, oversized shirts, long cotton dresses, and comfortable sandals. But some items are exclusive to my Bali trips and don't have a place in my Dubai looks. These include crop tops, jeans shorts, harem pants, and knitted beach dresses. I recognized that they wouldn't integrate into my Dubai wardrobe when I bought them. However, considering my frequent trips to Bali, I found the investment worthwhile.

You can save money and make the most of your vacation wardrobe by prioritizing articles that meet your needs and focusing on functional, timeless, and versatile pieces. A well-thought-out shopping approach ensures your purchases have long-term value beyond this trip.

Assembling

Chapter 5

Drawing Inspiration Cinema & Social Media

We live in an age when social media greatly influences our travels. As we research our destinations, we often turn to platforms like Instagram and Pinterest to gain insights into the appearance and style of a place. By exploring location tags and browsing through the posts of fellow travellers, we can discover the most photogenic spots, the trendiest restaurants, and the must-see landmarks. Hotels, cafes, and even entire towns have mastered creating picturesque settings, attracting millions of visitors each year with their carefully curated aesthetics and vibrant colour schemes.

Social media has become our trusted guidebook, revealing the most Instagrammable places and giving us a peek into the local fashion scene. With every scroll, a vibrant mosaic of expression reveals itself, where street style breathes the culture and spirit *du jour*.

When I scroll through Instagram, I like to look up geo-tagged posts of cities, popular restaurants, and iconic landmarks. I gather intel on the styling choices, materials, and colour schemes locals wear. I also see what clothes look completely out of place. By studying these examples, I train my eye to recognize what harmonises within a specific setting, sparking ideas and inspiration for my travel capsule.

I also love to analyse the architecture, colours, textures, and patterns of a destination. I aim to integrate these into my travel capsule, creating a visual symphony between my looks and the landscape of the destination. For example, in Bali, a lot of the temples and houses are built from volcanic rock, which is grey and turns darker with time. The nature in Bali is full of lush greenery, turquoise blue waters, white sands, and stunning sunsets. The local colour scheme provides ample guidance and inspiration for selecting colours that would complement these surroundings beautifully. This kind of harmony of colour in your outfits and the surrounding landscape is actually the key to Instagrammable travel-blogger-style photos.

Films are also a powerful source of inspiration and can help inform how we dress when travelling. Films can take us on a journey to different times and places and beautifully showcase local fashion. Not only can films inspire your travel capsule, but they can also offer a treasure trove of visual references for styling and accessorizing. For example, you might notice how a character layers an oversized blazer over a sweater or the artful draping of scarves

Inspiration

and the cock of a hat. These small details can bring a little *je ne sais quoi* to your travel style. Let's look at a couple of iconic destinations and see how we can embrace the local landscape and use references from films to inspire our travel capsule.

I love Italian cinema, and some of my favourite movies are set in Rome. In the 2013 film *La Grande Bellezza* director Paolo Sorrentino beautifully captures Rome's stunning architecture and acute fashion sense. The film opens with a fashion show held in a stunning palace overlooking the city, underscoring the importance of fashion and appearances. The models strut down the runway in gorgeous garments, each representing a different facet of Italian style, from the classic to the avant-garde.

The film's protagonist, Jep Gambardella, is seen wearing chic, tailored suits that exude a confident sophistication. The women in the film wear flowing, colourful dresses, elegant hats, and bold accessories. The city's vibrant street fashion is also featured, with characters wearing stylish sneakers, denim jackets, and graphic tees.

Another great example is the 1953 *Roman Holiday*, starring Audrey Hepburn and Gregory Peck. One of the most memorable scenes in the film is when Princess Ann (Audrey Hepburn) first meets Joe Bradley, played by Gregory Peck, and they take a scooter ride through the streets of Rome. Hepburn wears a white button-up blouse with a neck scarf tied around it, a full black skirt, and ballet flats. This iconic look captures the effortless chic of Italian fashion and fuses style and practicality. She wears various pieces that would look just as stylish today as they did in the 1950s. Her outfits showcase the classic Italian style, emphasising tailoring, high-quality fabrics, and timeless silhouettes.

During my first weekend trip to Rome, I drew inspiration from Princess Ann's classic style and chose an A-line dress paired

Inspiration

with chic flat sandals and a straw fedora for daytime exploration of the landmarks. As the evening descended, I changed into a floral print dress with a full midi-skirt complemented by red heels and a matching clutch. As I made my way down the street toward the opera house, I couldn't help but blush as I heard the enthusiastic cheers of the Roman men shouting *"Ma che bella!"*

In the more recent 2012 Woody Allen film *To Rome with Love*, the wardrobe design showcases a more contemporary Italian aesthetic. Arriving in Rome, Milly, played by Alison Pill, is dressed in a simple yet elegant cream-coloured dress that complements the city's warm, sun-bleached palette. She pairs the dress with a stylish crossbody purse in deep brown leather, contrasting nicely with the light-coloured dress. Milly's hair is swept up in a messy bun, lending a carefree and relaxed vibe to her overall look. Her look combines simplicity and elegance. She looks chic without being overdressed.

New York City is another timeless muse for filmmakers and a haven for fashion enthusiasts. From classic films like *Breakfast at Tiffany's* to contemporary gems like *Sex and the City*, the city that never sleeps has ignited trends, celebrated individuality, and shaped how we perceive and express our personal style. I remember Audrey Hepburn's elegant black dress and pearls as she gazes into Tiffany's window, forever etching the image of sophistication and glamour, and Carrie Bradshaw strutting down the streets of Manhattan in her iconic tutu skirt, defying conventions and inspiring a generation of street fashion.

Breakfast at Tiffany's is a film widely recognized for its role in defining New York fashion in the early 1960s. The film stars Audrey Hepburn as Holly Golightly, a country girl who desperately wants to belong in the creme de la creme of society. The film's iconic wardrobe, designed by Hubert de Givenchy, continues to inspire fashionistas to this day. One of the most memorable scenes in the movie is the opening where Holly steps out of a yellow cab, holding a paper bag in one hand and a coffee in the other. She wears a black dress, matching gloves, oversized sunglasses, and a pearl necklace. This look oozes the essence of New York style — simple, sophisticated with a coat of drama.

Another memorable fashion moment in the film is Holly's casual yet elegant outfit, consisting of black skinny trousers, a fitted turtleneck, and a long camel coat. I love this outfit as it's both practical and chic, perfect for strolling around New York City on a chilly day. This classic look served as my style inspiration during my work trips to New York City. On days out of the office, I'd wear black skinny jeans or leather leggings combined with a snug cashmere turtleneck and a long woollen coat, evoking the iconic Holly Golightly outfit.

Sex and the City is a TV series that ran from 1998 to 2004 and was later adapted into two movies. The impact of this show, and the costume designer Patricia Field's work, can't be overstated. It paved the way for the street style and individual expression through style around the world.

One of the most iconic moments is undoubtedly the opening sequence, where Carrie Bradshaw struts down the street in a tutu skirt and a simple white top. The tutu became an instant sensation, breaking all the rules and making a statement of New York City style: playful, unconventional, and always willing to take risks. In another episode, the girls attend a charity event, and Samantha Jones arrives in a white pantsuit with a plunging neckline, accessorized with a stunning diamond necklace. The look perfectly captures the essence of New York City style: a combination of high fashion and downtown cool.

Inspiration

During my business trips to New York City, I incorporated a touch of Carrie Bradshaw's whimsy. In addition to my usual black leather leggings and long coat, I wore a white embellished Angora sweater and a delightful beanie adorned with flowers. As the summer months rolled in, I fully embraced the spirit of Carrie Bradshaw by pairing stylish dresses with embellished heels for unforgettable nights in Manhattan. Lady luck smiled upon me when I had the opportunity to attend a Manolo Blahnik sample sale, an insider event which my local friends invited me to. I acquired a few pairs of iconic heels I still cherish and wear to this day.

So, my dear reader, as you embark on your next adventure, take a moment to indulge in the visual feast of the silver screen. Seek inspiration, insights, and styling tips from your favourite screen characters, and their stylists. Besides, who needs an excuse to re-watch iconic films with a fantastic wardrobe?

Inspiration

PART 2

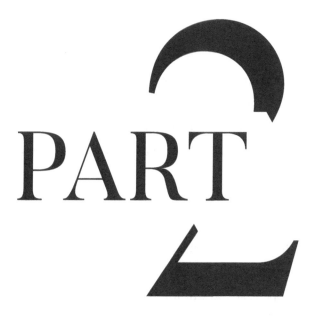

Destination Style Guide

Now, I will walk you through a detailed guide for twenty specific destinations, plus safari and skiing trips. For each destination, we will break down the three C's: climate, culture, and comfort, so you have the basics covered for planning your travel capsule. We will also look at the colour schemes and textures that work best at each destination. We'll touch upon traditional elements of fashion that you can incorporate for each location. Finally, I'll share packing recommendations for each destination. At the end of each section, there is a space where you can make notes. Use it to jot down details of your activities, reminders of items you want to take, additional pieces to buy, and whatever else comes to mind as you're reading.

These recommendations will serve as your stepping stone for packing. My goal is to provide you with a blueprint for a travel capsule that perfectly aligns with the demands and nuances of your travel destination while matching your personal style and preferences. I hope that you can use this as a base and curate your ideal travel capsule with confidence and ease for many trips to come.

Destination Style Guide

Bali

ali is an exotic island known for its picturesque rice paddies, lush greenery, thousands of temples, stunning sunsets, chic beach clubs, beautiful people, and a fascinating culture and history. There's so much to do in Bali that you may feel a little overwhelmed when it comes to packing. On a recent trip, I hiked a volcano, went island hopping and snorkelling, went to yoga and breathwork classes, got massages, visited waterfalls, dined at upscale restaurants, spent an afternoon at a beach club, wandered through rice paddies and visited temples. My trip lasted three weeks, and I had a small and functional capsule that worked for all these occasions. Before you pack, have an idea of what you plan to do and which parts of the island you will visit, so that you have the right clothes for each type of activity.

There's a mix of styles across the island. Traditional Balinese outfits are colourful and often beautifully embroidered. Many women wear the traditional Balinese sarong with a shirt or T-shirt. But many locals wear Western clothing, especially the younger generation. Bali is also a favourite destination for surfers and back-packers who walk around in shorts, harem pants, and singlets. There's also the chic yogi and wellness crew, which dresses in bohemian luxe. When dressing in Bali, aim for a relaxed and carefree look that will withstand the tropical weather, respect the culture, and allow you to enjoy the island vibe. Here's what to keep in mind when planning your Bali capsule.

Climate

Bali has a tropical climate with warm and humid weather throughout the year. The average temperature ranges from 25°C (77°F) to 30°C (86°F), and the island experiences two distinct seasons: the dry season (April to September) and the wet season (October to March). The humidity in Bali can be very high, ranging anywhere from 80% to 97% during the wet season. So, the heat feels much more intense and sticky. Packing lightweight and breathable clothing, which allows for air circulation and keeps you fresh during the day, is essential to stay comfortable in this high heat and humidity.

That said, Bali has microclimates with unique weather conditions that can vary significantly from one part of the island to another. The coastal regions generally experience a tropical climate with high humidity and warm temperatures year-round. However, the central highlands can be much, much colder, especially during the rainy season from November to March. Bring warm clothes if you're visiting Ubud, Mount Agung, Mount Batur, or the lakes. For trips to these areas, layering becomes key as temperatures change drastically throughout the day and drop significantly when it rains. Include a shawl, a light sweater or hoodie, and a lightweight rain jacket.

Bali

Culture

Balinese culture is rich in traditions and spirituality. Modesty is highly valued, and it is customary to cover the shoulders and knees, particularly when visiting temples and sacred sites. Opt for a full-length dress or loose trousers with a loose shirt. If you have the luck to participate in one of Balinese traditional ceremonies, wear a white shirt, shorts, and a traditional sarong that looks like a full-length skirt when tied around the waist. If you don't own one, you can easily pick one out when you get there.

On the other hand, parts of Bali are very international and have become home to many bloggers, digital nomads, and creative entrepreneurs. In areas like Canggu, Seminyak, Ubud, and Uluwatu, it is common to see crop tops and hot pants. While highly tourist areas are pretty liberal when it comes to showing skin, it's better to dress more modestly if you explore the capital Denpasar, or head to less cosmopolitan parts of the island.

Comfort

Loose-fitting clothing, such as kaftans, maxi dresses, loose trousers, and flowy tops will keep you fresh and comfortable in tropical weather. It's likely that you will sweat and feel very sticky during the day. You may find yourself changing clothes several times a day, so take enough to rotate at least two outfits per day. Don't panic when you read this. Laundry is cheap and available everywhere.

Layering crop tops with an oversized shirt, kaftan, or kimono is a great way to keep cool and protect your skin from the midday sun. Scooters are the most popular mode of transportation around

Bali

the island, and there isn't much walking in the cities. So, you can count on flip-flops or comfortable sandals for daily footwear. When it comes to dressing up for the evening, pair your evening wear with a pair of leather slides or sandals. I wouldn't go as far as packing heels, but if you must add some height, opt for a pair of wedges.

Colour scheme

Bali is known for its vibrant and colourful atmosphere. Embrace the island's kaleidoscope and incorporate a variety of vibrant hues into your travel capsule. Think of shades inspired by the natural surroundings, including ocean blues, lush greens, sunset oranges and purples, and rich floral prints. If you're not a fan of bright colours, go for earthy shades of brown and beige or white, grey, and black which will look minimalistic and chic in the Balinese landscape.

Textures

Given the warm and humid climate, prioritize comfortable and breathable fabrics such as cotton, linen, and lightweight blends. Consider incorporating textures like woven details, crochet, or embroidered accents. Embrace the organic feel of Bali by choosing materials that evoke a sense of nature and relaxation.

Must-haves

When packing for Bali, include essentials such as:

Bali

Clothing

- Lightweight sundresses
- Midi or maxi skirt
- Lightweight, loose trousers
- Comfortable shorts
- Breathable tops (tank tops, crop tops, T-shirts)
- Oversized linen or cotton shirt
- Sweater or hoodie
- Sportswear (hiking and yoga)
- Swimwear
- Rash guard (if surfing)
- Kaftan or cover up
- Light rain-proof jacket

Footwear

- Sandals or slides
- Flip-flops
- Trainers or hiking boots (if hiking)

Accessories

- Wide-brimmed hat or cap
- Sunglasses
- Tote or beach bag
- Backpack (if hiking)

Bali

Good to have

Consider bringing a lightweight shawl, a reusable water bottle, mosquito repellent, a waterproof phone case for water activities. It's also a good idea to include a waterproof bag and a plastic envelope to protect your documents from humidity. Also, stock up on good quality sunscreen because it's expensive and hard to find in Bali.

Traditional fashion elements to consider

Traditional Balinese fashion is known for its intricate prints, embroidery, and handcrafted accessories. You can incorporate elements of Balinese style into your outfits by opting for batik prints, ikat weaves, or traditional kebaya-inspired tops. Accessorize with locally made jewellery or carry a handwoven bag. Decorate your hair with the fragrant frangipani flowers, which are ubiquitous on the island. Check our Bali Collection on Pinterest for inspiration for your outfits. Search for @travelwithstylecollection in the home search bar to find our curated boards.

Bali

NOTES

_____

_____

_____

_____

_____

_____

_____

_____

_____

_____

_____

_____

_____

_____

Bali

Bangkok

Bangkok is one of the most popular tourist destinations in the world, known for its busy markets, delicious street food, zooming tuk-tuks, and elaborate temples. It is a mix of bright colours, intricate patterns, and a complex blend of old and new. Dressing "appropriately" in Bangkok ultimately depends on where you're going and what you're doing. Wearing a kimono and flip-flops on a temple visit is appropriate, but wearing this on a night out will look out of place. Regardless of the location, dressing respectfully in Bangkok is essential. Here's what to keep in mind when planning your capsule to Bangkok.

Climate

Bangkok has a tropical monsoon climate. This means high temperatures and high humidity throughout the year. It experiences three distinct seasons: hot, rainy, and mild. The hot season lasts from

March to June, with temperatures often reaching over 35°C (95°F). The rainy season falls between July and October, bringing frequent showers and high humidity. From November to February, you'll find slightly milder temperatures ranging from 20 to 30°C (68-86°F). Given these conditions, opt for breathable and moisture-wicking clothes that will keep you fresh and dry. The sun in Bangkok is extreme, so take extra precautions to protect your skin on this trip. Ensure you have long-sleeved shirts, long trousers, and skirts, and consider UV protection clothing. It's also worth mentioning that many public places, such as malls, cinemas, and many hotels, will have blasting air-conditioning. It's good to bring along a shawl to wrap up for these situations.

Culture

The Thai people value politeness and modesty. It's important to show respect for their culture. If you plan on visiting the temples during your trip to Bangkok, dress modestly. Avoid tight clothing, spaghetti straps, crop tops, miniskirts, and shorts. Make sure to cover your shoulders and knees. On my first trip to Bangkok, I came unprepared without long trousers. So, I purchased a pair of long, cotton pants with a Thai motif at the local market to wear around town during the daytime. Most temples in Bangkok have a shoes-off policy. Bring a pair of bright-coloured flip-flops or slip-on sandals, which you can easily spot in the sea of shoes on your way out. You may wear a hat and sunglasses to the temples. You may also use a scarf to cover your head.

On the other hand, Bangkok has a vibrant party scene. Most famous rooftop bars are an elevated experience (pun intended), so a smart casual dress code is in place for most of them. Ditch the flip-flops and loose trousers for a sexy dress or a skirt with a silk blouse paired with heels when heading for a night out. But there are plenty of nightlife spots where a casual dress code is acceptable. You will see locals and tourists alike having a drink in shorts, T-shirts, and crop tops. Check out the photos of the place you're going to on Google or Instagram in advance to gauge what dress code is appropriate.

Comfort

Due to the hot and humid climate, lightweight and breathable clothing is essential for comfort in Bangkok. You will probably get a Thai massage at least once, which happens with clothes on. Wear clothes that allow unrestricted movement, such as yoga pants or Thai fishermen's trousers for the massage. These are adjustable, one-size-fits-all pants that fold and tie around your waste. They are perfect for the massage and can double as loungewear after.

Flip-flops are ideal when visiting Bangkok. Since many places are shoes-off. If you prefer closed footwear, opt for slip-on shoes such as mules, ballerinas, or trainers with no laces. If you're visiting during the rainy season, pack anti-skid rubber shoes. Bring along a pair of nice heels or wedges if you plan to go out.

Colour scheme

Symbolism and colour are an important part of Thai Culture, and there are a lot of nuances when it comes to colour. In fact, in Thailand, there's a colour for every day of the week! This tradition is

Bangkok

no longer popular among the younger generation. However, many traditional Thais still know the colours and when to wear them. If you're interested in following this, here's a quick breakdown. Red for Sunday, yellow for Monday, pink for Tuesday, green for Wednesday, orange for Thursday, light blue for Friday, and purple for Saturday.

Black and white are only worn to a funeral. Black is associated with bad luck, so it is best to avoid it. The Thai people avoid wearing blue on Sundays. On Mondays, locals steer clear of red. That said, Thai people are very open-minded about most things, and the colour you wear during your visit isn't going to be an issue. Take inspiration from Bangkok's lively atmosphere and incorporate bold and bright colours like tropical blues, fiery oranges, and rich greens into your capsule. During the day, wear light colours that reflect the sun. Don't shy away from playful patterns and prints that reflect the city's energy and spirit.

Textures

Embrace lightweight and airy textures to combat the heat and humidity in Bangkok. Opt for fabrics like cotton, linen, and rayon during the day. A breathable linen dress will serve you tirelessly on a trip to Bangkok! You can also wear moisture-wicking fabrics and UV-protection clothing if you have sensitive skin. Polyester and nylon are saviours during the rainy season thanks to their quick-drying ability. Avoid jeans as they are heavy, hot, and take forever to dry. Incorporate a few silk items to dress up in the evening. Textured elements such as embroidered details or woven fabrics can add depth to your evening outfits.

Bangkok

Must-haves

A few essential items to include in your Bangkok travel capsule are:

Clothing

- T-shirts, tank tops
- Lightweight blouse
- Breathable and loose trousers
- Light and airy midi or maxi dress
- Midi skirt
- Long-sleeved oversized shirt
- Pair of comfortable shorts
- Yoga pants
- Swimwear
- Coverup or sarong
- Trousers from quick-dry synthetics (rainy seasons)
- Light rain-proof jacket (rainy season)

Footwear

- Anti-slip waterproof shoes (rainy season)
- Closed flat shoes such as ballet flats, espadrilles or sneakers
- Dress shoes for upscale restaurants and clubs

Bangkok

Accessories

- Hat or cap
- Sunglasses
- Crossbody bag with zip
- Backpack (day trips)
- Clutch (evenings out)
- Shawl or pashmina

Good to have

Consider packing a lightweight kimono for visiting temples. A foldable tote bag for carrying impromptu shopping and souvenirs, a reusable water bottle, and a compact umbrella. It's a good idea to bring a waterproof pouch for electronics and documents when travelling during the rainy season.

Traditional fashion elements to consider

You can incorporate aspects of the Thai aesthetic into your look with intricate embroidery, silk items, or traditional Thai patterns and motifs. A full-length *pha sinh*, a traditional skirt combined with long-sleeved silk blouses, is a staple for Thai women. Consider wearing it with a white T-shirt and flip-flops for exploring temples. Also, incorporate Thai-inspired accessories like beaded jewellery or woven bags into your looks. Check our Bangkok Collection on Pinterest for inspiration for your outfits. Search for @travelwithstylecollection in the home search bar to find our curated boards.

Bangkok

NOTES

Barcelona

Barcelona is a captivating city that blends breathtaking architecture, a rich history, bold and innovative design, and an unshakeable *joie de vivre*. It's a beloved tourist destination, particularly in the summer months. When it comes to dressing, Barcelona is a great place to let your personality shine! There are no restrictions on what you can wear. The key to dressing for Barcelona is outfits that are based on classic, well-tailored pieces, but have a little bit of eclectic edge. In fact, this where you can showcase your quirkiest pieces. During my stay in Barcelona, I thoroughly enjoyed sporting graphic prints, funky coats, chunky boots, and statement accessories. Your travel capsule for Barcelona will mostly be influenced by the season. Here's what you need to know when packing for Barcelona.

Climate

Barcelona experiences a Mediterranean climate with mild, humid winters and hot, dry summers. The temperature in summer is highs of 29°C (84°F) and lows of 22°C (71°F). When visiting Barcelona during the summer, ensure you bring lightweight and breathable clothing. A classic summer wrap dress is an ideal piece to transition from daytime sightseeing to sipping sangrias in the evening. A jumpsuit is another great option for the summer weather. Pair them with a pair of espadrilles or block-heel sandals.

In the spring, temperatures average between 17-23°C (62-73°F). Bring along a pair of jeans that can be dressed up or dressed down and don't forget warm layers. Since Barcelona is quite edgy, ripped and distressed jeans work well. A bright scarf is a great way to add a pop of colour to your outfits. Opt for closed shoes such as leather trainers or ankle boots. For the evenings, opt for a pair of boots with a chunky heel.

In early autumn, temperatures range between 26°C (78°F) and 17°C (62°F). However, in November it cools down to 17°C - 8°C (62°F - 46°F). A trusted pair of dark jeans paired with comfortable ankle boots will be a good base for your outfits. A knit dress paired with warm opaque or patterned tights and a warm coat is another elegant option.

During winter, temperatures hover between 13°C (55°F) and 4°C (40°F). Pack warm layers. Long-sleeved tops, cosy sweaters, sweater dresses. Bring a warm coat, hat, and gloves. In terms of shoes, go for ankle booties or tall, riding-inspired boots. The good news is that there is no snow! However, due to the humidity and winds, the winter chill cuts to the bone, so be prepared!

Barcelona

Culture

Barcelona is a beautiful blend of tradition and modernity, honouring creative and bold spirits. Feel free to bring along outfits that reflect your unique style. The locals tend to dress in smart casual wear with a touch of bohemian flair and eccentricity. Obviously, ensure you have modest clothing options for visiting churches and cathedrals. This means covering your shoulders and knees. Long trousers or an elegant dress will do the trick.

Comfort

Barcelona is the type of city where you can leave your accommodation in the morning and explore all day. On a typical day, you may be taking the subway, waiting in lines at busy tourist attractions, wandering through museums and romantic neighbourhoods, and sitting down for food and drinks at one of the many tapas bars before heading out to an upscale restaurant Your outfits will work best if they can take you from day to night.

Bring comfortable footwear, such as sneakers, boots, or sandals, depending on the season. Keep in mind that the city's terrain can be hilly, and the old town is paved with cobblestones. So, heels are not advisable. Go for flats or shoes with a small, block heel. My go-to footwear during the winter and spring were a pair of dark red Dr Martens and white leather sneakers. When summer arrived, I opted for simple leather sandals with a slight heel and leather espadrilles.

Word of warning: Barcelona is infamous for pickpockets. Ensure your bag allows you to securely carry your valuables when sightseeing. Finally, include layers to adjust to the changing temperatures throughout the day.

Barcelona

Colour scheme

Pack a mix of bold colours like orange, red, yellow, blue, and green. Embrace graphic and floral prints, colour blocking, and contrasts. In the winter months, go for muted hues like Bordeaux, ruby red, sapphire, and dark greens. If bold colours are not your cup of cava, opt for neutral tones like white, beige, olive green, and navy.

Textures

For the summer months, focus on breathable and lightweight materials such as cotton, linen, rayon, and silk. For winter, include warmer fabrics like wool, cashmere, and technical blends to keep you cosy and insulated. Consider thermal tops and leggings as your base layer. A faux fur coat will keep you warm and looking stylish.

Must-haves

Some essentials to pack for Barcelona include:

Summer

Clothing
• Lightweight shirt
• T-shirts and tops
• Skirt or shorts
• Linen or cotton trousers
• Breathable dress

Barcelona

- Romper or jumpsuit
- Swimwear

Footwear

- Comfortable espadrilles or sandals
- Beach flip-flops

Accessories

- Sunglasses
- Wide-brimmed hat
- Crossbody or tote bag

Winter

Clothing

- Warm sweaters
- Warm trousers
- Dark jeans
- Long sweater dress
- Long sleeve shirts and blouses
- Warm overcoat
- Opaque tights
- Warm socks

Barcelona

Footwear

- Comfortable, waterproof shoes or boots
- Comfortable sneakers

Accessories

- Warm hat
- Warm scarf
- Warm gloves
- crossbody bag

Autumn/ Spring:

Clothing

- Lightweight long-sleeved tops
- Light sweaters or cardigans for layering
- Long-sleeved dresses
- Trousers or jeans
- Skirt
- Light jacket or trench coat

Footwear

- Comfortable walking shoes or sneakers
- Waterproof boots
- Casual dress shoes for evenings

Barcelona

Accessories

- Scarf

- Light gloves (early spring and late autumn)

- Crossbody bag

Good to have

Consider bringing shawl or pashmina for visiting religious sites, a reusable water bottle to stay hydrated, and a compact umbrella, in case of a rain shower.

Traditional fashion elements

Incorporate traditional Spanish and Catalan elements into your outfits. Polka dot prints, flamenco-inspired off-the-shoulder dresses, tops with frills, statement jewellery with natural stones, espadrilles, and a straw hat will all look great in Barcelona! Check our Barcelona Collection on Pinterest for inspiration for your outfits. Search for @ travelwithstylecollection in the home search bar to find our curated boards.

Barcelona

NOTES

Beijing

eijing is known as much for its bold, modern architecture as its ancient sites, such as the grand Forbidden City and the Imperial Palace. The city offers visitors no shortage of experiences to indulge in. When planning a trip to Beijing, it's essential to consider factors such as the diverse climate, cultural nuances, and what activities you will be doing.

Climate

Beijing experiences four distinct seasons. Summers are hot and humid, with temperatures reaching around 30°C (86°F) or more. Winters are cold and dry, with temperatures dropping below freezing and occasional snowfall. Spring and autumn offer mild and pleasant weather but can have temperature fluctuations. Pack casual, lightweight layers that you can add and subtract during this season. Light wool is a good choice as it naturally helps to regulate your body temperature. A light raincoat is helpful during the rainy seasons of May, June, July, and August.

Culture

The Chinese are conservative. Beijing is fashionable and has adopted the Western style, but you rarely find a Chinese woman older than a teenager in jeans. It's better to leave shorts and revealing tops at home. When visiting temples or religious sites, dress modestly, covering your shoulders and knees. Trousers are a must since many temples will forbid entry to women wearing skirts. Outside of religious sites, casual clothes are generally acceptable. If you are taking swimwear, opt for a one-piece rather than a bikini.

Comfort

Beijing is a bustling city with much walking and sightseeing. Comfortable footwear is crucial. Opt for a trusted pair of boots, flats, or sneakers that provide good support and are broken in. Don't expect to buy shoes in China! The average Chinese person has far smaller feet than the average Westerner, so you may not find any to fit.

Colour scheme

In terms of colour scheme, neutrals, and earth tones are versatile and blend well with Beijing's urban landscape. Consider shades of beige, grey, black, and white as a base. Add pops of colour with accessories or statement pieces. Don't shy away from bright colours, especially red, which is considered lucky.

Beijing

Textures

Opt for breathable fabrics such as cotton, linen, and rayon during the summer months. Add warmer textures such as leather, wool, and technical fabrics during the shoulder seasons and winter. Elevate your outfits with textures such as silk, velvet, brocade, or jacquard, which reflect the city's cultural influences.

Must-haves

Some essential items to pack for Beijing include

Summer

Clothing

- Lightweight blouses, shirts, and tops
- Linen or cotton trousers
- Capri pants or shorts
- Lightweight oversize shirt
- Lightweight dress below the knees

Footwear

- Comfortable sandals
- Flip-flops
- Dress shoes for evenings

Beijing

Accessories

- Sunglasses
- Hat
- Crossbody or tote bag
- Light shawl

Winter

Clothing

- Warm jacket or coat
- Sweaters
- Thermal underlayers
- Warm trousers
- Long, knitted dress
- Warm socks

Footwear

- Comfortable, waterproof footwear
- Dress shoes for formal occasions

Accessories

- Warm hat
- Warm scarf

Beijing

- Warm gloves
- Crossbody bag or tote

Autumn/ Spring

Clothing

- Long-sleeved tops
- Trousers
- Midi-skirt
- Long-sleeved dresses
- Sweaters and cardigans
- Versatile, medium-weight jacket

Footwear

- Comfortable shoes or boots
- Dress shoes for formal occasions

Accessories

- Crossbody bag or tote
- Scarf
- Sunglasses

Beijing

Good to have

Pack a pantsuit or an elegant dress for a more formal dinner or if you have plans to visit the opera or concerts. Bring a shawl or a pashmina to keep you warm and as a modesty cover. An umbrella is useful, but buy one when you get there, they are readily available and cheap.

Traditional fashion elements to consider

Consider incorporating elements like Mandarin collars, qipao dresses, or cheongsam-inspired blouses into your outfits. Embrace elegant and tailored garments with sleek silhouettes. Accessorise with traditional-inspired jewellery, such as jade or pearl. Have a look at our Beijing Collection on Pinterest for inspiration. Search for @travelwithstylecollection in the home search bar to find our curated boards.

Beijing

NOTES

Beijing

Berlin

During the twentieth century, Berlin established itself as a liberal Mecca. It drew the creative, rebellious, and artistic types, who continue to shape Berlin's unique cultural climate. While Berlin has changed dramatically in the last decades, Berliners still visibly enjoy their freedom by clearly expressing their style.

Climate

Berlin experiences a temperate seasonal climate, with warm summers and cold winters. Summers are generally mild with temperatures ranging from 20°C to 30°C (68°F to 86°F). The weather can change throughout the day, so always bring layers. Winters are cold, with temperatures often dropping below freezing, averaging around -1°C to 4°C (30°F to 39°F).

Culture

Berlin has a relaxed and casual vibe. Berlin's liberal attitudes extend towards dress codes, you can wear whatever you want. With a very anything-goes attitude, the motto is "Express yourself." Feel free to wear whatever you're most comfortable in. The locals will appreciate your expression of personal style. Most Berlin clubs here don't have a dress code, so don't worry about getting dressed up to go party. The only local tip that can help you get into the notoriously picky Berghain club is to wear black.

Comfort

Comfortable clothing and shoes are indispensable for exploring Berlin's landmarks and neighbourhoods. Opt for versatile and relaxed pieces that allow easy movement. However, avoid wearing sweatpants or activewear when exploring the city (unless it's vintage Adidas, see below). Of course, bring active clothes if you plan to run and exercise in Berlin's parks.

Berlin

Colour scheme

"Berliners wear black" is the conventional wisdom. However, arriving in the city, you will find this is hardly true. Berliners embrace colour in their looks. You'll find people wearing everything from classic black to vibrant street-style-inspired outfits. Choose colours that reflect your style and make you feel confident.

Textures

Berliners appreciate a mix of textures in their looks. Embrace layers and experiment with different fabrics such as cotton, denim, wool, nylon, polyester, and leather, depending on what the season permits.

Must-haves

Summer

Clothing

- Classy, relaxed sundress
- Linen or cotton trousers
- Shorts or skirts
- T-shirts or blouse
- Cardigan or hoodie
- Light jacket

Footwear

- Comfortable sandals
- Sneakers or closed toe shoes

Accessories

- Light scarf
- Sunhat or cap

Berlin

- Tote, crossbody bag or backpack
- Sunglasses

Winter

Clothing

- Warm sweaters
- Thermal underlayers
- Long-sleeve tops and shirts
- Warm trousers
- Long knitted dress
- Warm jacket or long coat
- Warm socks

Footwear

- Warm, waterproof boot

Accessories

- Large statement scarf
- Opaque tights
- Warm hat
- Warm gloves
- Tote, crossbody bag, or backpack
- Umbrella

Berlin

Spring/Autumn

Clothing

- Long sleeve shirts or tops
- Sweater or cardigan
- Jeans or trousers
- Versatile, medium-weight jacket

Footwear

- Comfortable walking shoes or boots
- Waterproof shoes

Accessories

- Statement scarf
- Gloves (late autumn)
- Sunglasses
- Tote, crossbody bag or backpack
- Umbrella

Berlin

Good to have

If you plan to dine in upscale restaurants or attend a special event, pack at least one sophisticated outfit. Opt for a blazer over a cocktail dress or a tailored suit. Since Berlin is a bike-friendly city and offers many parks, bring activewear if you plan on cycling or jogging.

Traditional fashion elements to consider

Incorporate aspects of Berlin's street style, such as oversized pieces, vintage finds, and edgy accessories, into your looks. You'll see that 80s vintage sportswear is an obsession in Berlin. If you can find yourself some classic Adidas or some grunge-era relics, you will be all set. The flea markets on Sunday mornings all across the city are the best spots to find some vintage pieces. Have a look at our Berlin Collection on Pinterest for inspiration! Search for @travelwithstyle-collection in the home search bar to find our curated boards.

Berlin

NOTES

Berlin

Bora Bora & French Polynesia

Bora Bora, known as the "Pearl of the Pacific," is a tropical paradise nestled in the heart of French Polynesia. It's renowned for stunning natural beauty and overwater bungalows that beckon honeymooners from around the world. Whether you will be lounging on the pristine beaches, scuba diving, going on nature trails, or indulging in delectable cuisine, Bora Bora offers an idyllic setting for creating unforgettable memories. Here's what to keep in mind when packing for Bora Bora.

Climate

Bora Bora enjoys a tropical climate with warm temperatures ranging from 25°C (77°F) to 30°C (86°F) throughout the year. The temperature may vary slightly depending on the season, but you can generally expect pleasant and balmy temperatures during your visit. The weather is hot and humid, so bring lightweight and breathable clothing to stay comfortable.

Culture

Bora Bora is a blend of Polynesian culture, which emphasises simplicity and respect, and Western influence. Missionaries and Christianity influenced local traditions and customs in many areas. So, first-time visitors to Polynesia are often astonished at the intensity of the islanders' devotion to Christianity. While you'll likely spend most of your days wearing swimwear in your resort, dress modestly in loose-fitting clothes that cover your shoulders and knees when visiting local villages or landmarks.

Comfort

Pack comfortable walking shoes and breathable sportswear for hiking and exploring the island's lush landscapes. Remember to bring multiple swimsuits and cover-ups for lounging on the beach. Take lightweight dresses with a relaxed fit or two-piece co-ord sets to roam around the hotel and visit the spa and the restaurants. Flat sandals, sliders, and espadrilles will be perfect for walking around the resort.

Colour scheme

Embrace the tropical landscape of Bora Bora with shades that complement the island's natural beauty. From turquoise to lush greens, to the kaleidoscope of flower prints. If you prefer a more neutral look, opt for white, creme, and ochre for your outfits and swimwear.

Textures

Embrace lightweight and breezy fabrics that allow airflow and keep you fresh in the island's tropical climate. Look for breathable materials like cotton, linen, and silk that offer comfort and elegance. Level up your style with sandals adorned with pearls, shells, and colourful pom poms.

Must-haves

Clothing

- Fresh and summery dresses
- Co-ord sets in relaxed silhouettes
- Multiple swimsuits
- Beach cover-ups
- Lightweight and breathable tops
- Shorts or skirt
- Light shawl or cardigan
- Breathable sports shoes for hiking
- Breathable and moisture wicking sportswear

Bora Bora

Footwear

- Sandals
- Flip-flops
- Casual dress shoes for dinners

Accessories

- Statement accessories
- Wide-brimmed hat
- Sunglasses

Bora Bora

Good to have

Consider packing a waterproof phone pouch or camera housing to capture the mesmerising underwater scenes, your own snorkelling gear and rash guards, and a lightweight rain jacket for the occasional tropical shower. Also, consider taking aqua shoes to protect your feet on rocky or hot surfaces.

Traditional fashion elements to consider

Incorporating traditional elements of Polynesian culture such as the pāreu or pareo. This is a wraparound skirt typically worn in Tahiti or other Pacific islands. Wear it as a skirt or a beach cover-up. The shopping in Bora Bora offers a wealth of local specialties — like expertly woven baskets and beautiful strings of pearls for your outfits. Have a look at our Bora Bora Collection on Pinterest for inspiration. Search for @travelwithstylecollection in the home search bar to find our curated boards.

Bora Bora

NOTES

Bora Bora

Cambodia

C ambodia beckons travellers with its enchanting temples, lush landscapes, and warm-hearted people. From the awe-inspiring Angkor Wat to the bustling streets of Phnom Penh, there is a lot to admire. To ensure you have the best time and avoid wardrobe faux pas, follow the simple tips below.

Climate

Cambodia has a tropical climate characterized by two main seasons: the dry and rainy seasons. The dry season, which runs from October to April, brings hot and humid temperatures. The rainy season, from May to September, is characterized by frequent showers and high humidity. So natural fabrics like linen, cotton, and silk will keep you cooler, while lightweight, loose-fitting cotton items (such as long-sleeved trousers and shirts) will protect against mosquitoes and the sun. Leave your jeans at home. It is way too hot for them.

Culture

Over 90% of the population in Cambodia follows Buddhism. The locals are gentle and bashful, and so is their clothing. Cambodians are used to foreign visitors, and shorts, skirts, camisoles, and singlets are popular with tourists and generally accepted. That said, modesty is highly valued. Avoid exposing your midriff or wearing micro-minis. Singlets and shorts are acceptable when visiting cities like Phnom Penh and Siem Reap. If you're travelling to more rural areas like Battambang or Kampong Cham, opt for a loose T-shirt or long-sleeved shirt and loose trousers.

Completely covering your legs and shoulders and wearing modest clothing are musts when visiting temples or other sacred sites. Most temples will require you to take off your shoes before entry. Bring a bright pair, which is easily spotted on the way out.

Comfort

Given the hot and humid climate, lightweight, breathable fabrics (such as cotton and linen) are your best friends. Loose-fitting clothing will also allow for better airflow and ease of movement. Sidewalks are often uneven, and many sites are unpaved, so bring comfortable walking shoes. A pair of lightweight walking boots with ankle support or sandals with a rugged bottom are a must. Also, pack a relaxing change of shoes like slides or flip-flops.

Colour scheme

Embrace Cambodia's vibrant and lively atmosphere by incorporating warm oranges, lush greens, and rich blues, into your outfits.

Cambodia

Additionally, neutral tones such as white, stone, brown, and creme can help you stay fresh and harmonize with the landscape.

Textures

Fabrics like cotton, linen, and silk are breathable and always elegant. Breathable blends like rayon also work well. Focus on fresh and flowy fabrics.

Must-haves

When packing for Cambodia, bring minimal clothing as laundry is cheap and easily accessible. These are your essentials:

Dry Season (October to April)

Clothing
■ Loose and breathable dress
■ Lightweight, breathable trousers
■ Long-sleeved shirt
■ T-shirts and singlets for layering
■ Swimwear
■ Cover-up (kaftan or sarong)
■ Lightweight scarf

Cambodia

Footwear

- Comfortable walking shoes
- Flip-flops

Accessories

- Hat
- Sunglasses
- Crossbody bag
- Backpack for daily excursions

Wet Season (May to September)

Clothing

- Quick-drying, loose trousers
- Quick-drying, long-sleeved shirt
- T-shirts and singlets
- Swimming suit
- Cover-up (kaftan or sarong)
- Lightweight scarf
- Lightweight rain jacket or poncho

Footwear

- Waterproof sandals or shoes with good grip
- Flip flops

Cambodia

Accessories

- Hat
- Sunglasses
- Shawl
- Crossbody bag or backpack

Good to have

Bring insect repellent to protect yourself from mosquitoes, especially during the rainy season. Also, a compact umbrella can come in handy during unexpected showers. Consider packing waterproof pouches for electronics and important documents.

Traditional fashion elements to consider

Cambodia has a rich tradition of textiles and craftsmanship. Incorporate traditional elements such as scarves or wraps made from Cambodian silk, which showcase intricate designs and vibrant colours. Support local artisans by purchasing handmade jewellery or accessories. Have a look at our Cambodia Collection on Pinterest for inspiration! Search for @travelwithstylecollection in the home search bar to find our curated boards.

Cambodia

NOTES

Cambodia

Cancun & Riviera Maya

This Cancun packing list also works for other destinations in the Riviera Maya, including Tulum, Akumal, Playa del Carmen, and Bacalar. There is so much to see and do here! Whether you are the adventurous type and plan to see natural wonders and archaeological sites, or if you're more into the beach, cocktail-in-hand holiday, your Cancun travel capsule will depend on your activities.

Climate

Cancun and Tulum have a tropical climate, so it's hot and humid throughout the year. Average temperatures range from around 26°C

(79°F) to 32°C (90°F) during the day. The evenings are fresh, averaging between 19°C (66°F) and 26°C (79°F). The wettest months are June to October. Light layers in natural fabrics like cotton, silk, linen, and wool will work well here. The air-conditioning in hotels and restaurants can be fierce, and the sea breeze can be chilly. Bring cardigan or light sweater. At night, you might need a light jacket or sweater in the winter months. Finally, you may experience some drizzle or a sudden downpour, so a lightweight pack-away raincoat or travel umbrella will be handy.

Culture

Mexico has a rich cultural heritage! Respectful attire is appreciated when visiting religious sites or participating in cultural events. Opt for a midi or maxi dress, lightweight linen trousers, and a blouse. Ensure you have a shawl or scarf that can be used as a cover-up, especially when entering sacred places. Avoid wearing tops that reveal your stomach or cleavage. If you plan to venture outside the popular resort areas, use your midi or maxi skirts or dresses, lightweight trousers, or Capri trousers rather than shorts.

On the other hand, the resorts have a laid-back vibe, so think flowy skirts, rompers, caftans, and off-the-shoulder dresses with sandals. Wear your swimwear for the beach and pool and use a sarong or sundress to cover up for breakfast or lunch. Dinners at resorts tend to be smart casual, but some restaurants will not allow shorts or camisoles. Bring a selection of sundresses and skirts, which you can style with sandals.

Comfort

Pack some comfortable closed-toe walking shoes or sneakers for exploring outside the resort. The ground at the Mayan ruins of Tulum and other sites can be bumpy and dusty. Also, if you get to climb the pyramids, they are steep and slippery when wet. Make sure to pack shoes with a good grip. Bring a pair of comfortable sandals for the resort and a pair of flip-flops or slides for the beach and pool. If you plan to get around town by bike, include some comfy shorts or rompers.

Colour scheme

Usually, the colours of traditional Mexican dress are red, brown, green, and yellow. Embrace the traditional colours by opting for clothes in earthy browns, rich greens, and shades of yellow and red. White, straw, and sand will also serve as excellent base colours for your capsule.

Textures

Use lightweight fabrics such as cotton, linen, and silk for your looks. Add textures such as straw or wool to add depth to your outfits.

Cancun & Riviera Maya

Must-haves

Clothing

- Swimwear
- Cover-ups (kaftans or sarongs)
- Flowy sundresses
- Rompers
- Co-ord set for lounging
- Comfy shorts
- Lightweight and breathable tops
- Capri trousers
- Light cardigan or shawl

Footwear

- Sandals or leather slides
- Flip-flops
- Comfortable closed shoes with good traction

Accessories

- Cross-body bag
- Clutch
- Straw bag or beach tote
- Wide-brimmed hat
- Sunglasses

Cancun & Riviera Maya

Good to have

A few simple accessories or a piece of statement jewellery will help you glam up for dinner. I also recommend taking a dry pouch for your phone and keys on expeditions to the Cenotes. Bring a head-lamp for biking or flashlight for walking at night as there are often no streetlights. Also, include a waterproof phone case to protect your phone and ear plugs and a sleep mask (if you like to sleep in or the sounds of the beach or jungle might keep you awake). Lastly, pack a refillable water bottle for a day out or hiking, and a battery pack (if your hotel has limited hours of electricity).

Traditional fashion elements to consider

Mexican national clothing is very bright and beautiful. The main characteristics of Mexican national attire are sun protection, bright-ness, and moderate modesty. *Quechquémitl* is a festive poncho worn for parties, holidays, and festivals. *Rebozo* is a shawl made from cotton, wool, or silk. The colour and pattern of the rebozo represent the region and community. Mexican skirts can be ankle-length or knee-length. They are typically made from cotton, wool, silk, and lace. Very often, they are wide, bright, and embroidered. Look for garments inspired by these traditional designs. Embrace the Mexican culture by incorporating classic features such as embroidery, lace, and beads into your looks. Also, look for items with prints of birds, flowers, animals, and geometric shapes. Accessorize with handmade jewellery or woven accessories that reflect the region's indigenous heritage. Have a look at our Cancun Collection on Pinterest for inspiration! Search for @travelwithstylecollection in the home search bar to find our curated boards.

Cancun & Riviera Maya

NOTES

_____

_____

_____

_____

_____

_____

_____

_____

_____

_____

_____

_____

_____

_____

_____

Cancun & Riviera Maya

Delhi & the Golden Triangle

India is an incredibly diverse and vibrant country that is continuously changing and growing every year. What visitors in India are expected to wear differs with location. Delhi is a big city, and you can get away with wearing more revealing clothing at your hotel, Western restaurants, pubs, and bars. However, Indian culture values modesty, so the conscious traveller should follow suit. Moreover, it's common to hear stories of unwarranted attention from strangers towards Western women dressed too provocatively for the local standards. To ensure that you avoid any unwelcome approaches, err on the side of caution and modesty. Regrettably, such encounters may occur irrespective of your clothing choices, and it's not confined to India alone. Nevertheless, I've heard many stories from fellow female travellers who faced considerable challenges in this regard during their solo trips to India.

Climate

Delhi experiences a hot, semi-arid climate with scorching summers, cold winters and a monsoon season. Summers can be sweltering, with temperatures soaring above 38°C (100°F) in peak months. Winters are chilly, with temperatures ranging from 7°C (45°F) to 24°C (75°F). The monsoon starts in July and lasts until mid-September, with temperatures between 25 °C (77 °F) on rainy days and 35–40 °C (95–104 °F) during dry spells. Pack lightweight and breathable clothing made from cotton or linen for summer and layer up with woollen sweaters and jackets for winter. Be mindful that the mornings and evenings can be very cold throughout the year, so it's a good idea to have a sweater or hoodie and a warm pair of socks. Full-sleeved clothes protect against sunburn during the day and mosquito bites at night. Jeans are popular, but they are too hot for the summer and take too long to dry during the monsoon. Finally, consider bringing some thermal underwear for winter.

Culture

India is very conservative. Unless you want to turn heads in public, leave your crop tops, mini-skirts, shorts, and tight or body-revealing clothes at home. It's best to avoid unwanted attention by dressing in clothes that cover both shoulders and knees. Think loose cotton shirts or T-shirts with flowy trousers or an ankle-length skirt. If you want to wear jeans, pair them with a kaftan or tunic. While visiting

Delhi

temples, gurudwara, or mausoleums, women must wear long skirts or trousers and have their shoulders covered. It is advisable to carry a light pashmina or scarf to wrap your head, as some religious places also require you to cover your hair.

Comfort

Delhi is crowded and bustling, so comfort is vital. Choose light-weight and loose-fitting clothing. Make sure to have some sturdy shoes since your feet will get dusty and dirty navigating the city's streets and attractions. It's best to avoid high heels. Bring a pair of flat sandals to change into in the evenings. During winter, you can opt for an elegant pair of flats or loafers.

Colour Scheme

Embrace Delhi's colourful atmosphere by incorporating bold and vibrant colours into your capsule. Traditional Indian outfits feature a variety of eye-catching hues: emerald green, saffron, canary, gold, and vermillion. So don't be afraid to experiment with colourful prints and patterns to blend in with the locals. Likewise, calming pastel shades like mint, sage, sand, and stone will look beautiful in the topography of the Golden Triangle.

Delhi

Textures

During the summer, focus on light, breathable clothing with cotton and linen. Opt for quick-drying fabrics during the monsoon season. Bring warm fabrics to keep you cosy during the early morning chills and the winter. Incorporate textures such as silk and chiffon and cotton with intricate embroidery into your outfits.

Must-haves

When deciding what to wear in India, remember to pack minimally – clothing and laundry are cheap.

Summer (March to June)

Clothing

- Loose cotton or linen trousers
- Several long-sleeved shirts
- Loose t-shirts
- Long dress or tunic
- Long skirt

Footwear

- Comfortable, breathable shoes or sandals
- Closed-toe shoes if you plan on doing a lot of walking

Accessories

- Sunhat
- Sunglasses
- Backpack or tote
- Light shawl or bandana

Delhi

Winter (November to February)

Clothing

- Warm sweater or hoodie
- Long-sleeve tops
- Loose, warm trousers
- Warm jacket
- Warm socks
- Jeans

Footwear

- Comfortable, closed toe shoes

Accessories

- Sunhat or cap
- Sunglasses
- Warm scarf
- Mittens
- Backpack or tote

Delhi

Monsoon (July to September)

Clothing

- Loose cotton or linen trousers
- Several long-sleeved shirts

- Loose t-shirts
- Long dress or tunic
- Long skirt
- Waterproof jacket or poncho

Footwear

- Comfortable, waterproof or sandals
- Flip-flops

Accessories

- Sunhat or cap
- Sunglasses
- Waterproof bag
- Light shawl or bandana

Delhi

Good to have

In India, you must go barefoot in most religious places. So, if you are concerned about getting your feet dirty, remember to bring several pairs of socks. If your hotel offers a pool or the beach, take swimwear with you as it's difficult and expensive to buy. If you are travelling by train, a lightweight scarf or sweater will come in handy, for the air-conditioning. For long or overnight journeys, you bring earplugs, an eye mask, your own toilet roll or baby wipes, and a cotton sleeper sheet. A portable charger or power bank, hand sanitiser, sunscreen, and insect repellent will be helpful during your trip.

Traditional fashion elements to consider

Delhi is renowned for its eclectic fashion. There are many traditional garments like *sarees, salwar kameez,* and *kurtas* that you can incorporate into your travel capsule. Many modern designers create minimalist and chic Kurtis (a co-ord of loose trousers and tunic). Incorporating elements of conventional Indian attire into your capsule can be a wonderful way to pay homage to the rich culture and dress to impress while respecting all cultural norms. Have a look at our Delhi Collection on Pinterest for inspiration. Search for @travelwithstylecollection in the home search bar to find our curated boards.

Delhi

NOTES

Delhi

Dubai

Dubai is the dazzling jewel of the United Arab Emirates and a playground of the finer things in life. Known for its extravagant architecture, world-class shopping, and upscale entertainment, Dubai is a destination that blends modernity with tradition. The city boasts some of the world's most luxurious malls, high-end designer boutiques and brands from around the globe, upscale dining, and once-in-a-lifetime experiences. Dubai is home to over 200 nationalities. It prides itself on being a place of tolerance and innovation. At the same time, it is still rooted in Islamic traditions. Here's what to keep in mind when packing for Dubai.

Climate

Dubai has a desert climate characterized by hot and arid conditions. Summers are scorching, with temperatures reaching well above

40°C (104°F), while winters are mild to warm with temperatures averaging 20-25°C (68-77°F). You may experience some showers and chilly winds in January and February. During the summer months, I recommend lightweight and breathable clothing for the daytime. During the winter months, bring a jumper, a versatile jacket, or raincoat. Surprisingly, the locals in Dubai also bring out their boots, jumpers, and jackets during the winter season. Due to the humidity, the evenings in January and February can feel quite cold. The first time I experienced winter in Dubai, I found myself layering everything I had to stay warm during the chilly nights. This is even more important if you're heading out to the desert for a safari, as temperatures can drop significantly after sunset. It is also worth noting the air-conditioning in most shopping malls, restaurants, hotels, and indoor attractions is glacial throughout the year! Have a shawl, cardigan, or blazer handy, so you can layer up as needed.

Culture

Dubai is a cosmopolitan city with a rich blend of cultures. Generally, most attires are accepted. You can wear a bikini (on the beach and in the pool), and you don't need to cover your hair. Generally, shorts, sexy dresses, camisoles, and crop tops are accepted in tourist areas. When visiting historical sites, museums, shopping malls, and business districts, it's advisable to cover your knees and shoulders. Also, when going on heritage tours and visiting the old part of Dubai, like the Al Fahidi district and the souks, dress conservatively to help avoid unwanted attention from the merchants. Opt for loose and breathable clothes that cover the shoulders, knees, and midriff. Capri trousers or linen trousers paired with a shirt, and leather slides will do nicely. You can also wear a midi-skirt with a blouse or an elegant dress.

Dubai

If you're planning to visit mosques, opt for a blouse or shirt with long sleeves, a long skirt or dress that covers the ankles, and a pashmina or shawl to wrap around your head. You can (but don't need to) wear an abaya. It's customary to dress up in the evenings, so glam up and bling out.

Comfort

One of the most popular activities when visiting Dubai is going on a desert safari. I recommend wearing a romper with long trousers or long, flowy trousers paired with a long-sleeved shirt. Length will offer protection from the sun during the day and keep you warmer at night. Temperatures drop drastically once the sun sets, so bring along a hoodie or sweater. Regarding footwear, I recommend wearing leather ankle walking boots or slides, which you can easily take off when you jump onto the dunes. Avoid wearing trainers because you will get so much sand in them! Otherwise, Dubai is a very comfortable and accessible city. Bring a pair of sandals or leather slides for the daytime and your favourite heels for the evenings.

Colour scheme

Dubai has a very modern and sleek aesthetic. Base your capsule on mutual tones like creme, white, sand, and stone or darker colours like brown and burnt ochre. You can also experiment with bold colours like yellow, orange, fuchsia, and green in your capsule to add a pop of colour. While too hot to wear during the day, black or dark shades of purple and blue are very popular colours for evening outfits.

Dubai

Textures

Regarding textures, lightweight and flowy fabrics are ideal for Dubai's warm weather. Consider fabrics like cotton, linen, chiffon, silk, and viscose. Embroidery, lace, and embellishments will add a touch of elegance to your looks. When going out to restaurants and bars, you can wear clothing from synthetic blends that provide more structure and warmth in the ubiquitous air-conditioning.

Must-haves

Here's what you need for a stylish and comfortable trip to Dubai

Clothing

- Midi skirts or dresses
- Capri trousers or long trousers
- Long-sleeve cotton shirt
- T-shirts and tops
- Swimwear
- Cover-ups
- Light cardigan or blazer
- Elegant evening dress
- Romper (desert)
- Sweater or hoodie (desert and winter)
- Warm jacket (winter)

Dubai

Footwear

- Comfortable sandals or leather slides
- Loafers or espadrilles
- Heels or dressy sandals
- Closed-toe shoes for formal occasions and venues
- Ankle Boots (desert and winter)

Accessories

- Shawl
- Sunhat
- Sunglasses
- Clutch for evenings
- Crossbody bag or tote
- Beach bag or basket

Dubai

Good to have

Because it's scorching during the day, a reusable water bottle and a fan come in handy while exploring the town. Also, pack plenty of sunscreens to protect your skin.

Traditional fashion elements to consider

Consider incorporating *kaftans*, *abayas*, or traditional Arabic-inspired clothing into your capsule. These can be found in local markets or boutiques, offering a unique and elegant touch to your looks. The city is also home to a burgeoning fashion scene. Why not treat yourself to a special fashion memento from one of the local shops? For inspiration, check out the Dubai Collection on Pinterest. Search for @travelwithstylecollection in the home search bar to find our curated boards.

Dubai

NOTES

Dubai

French Riviera

The French Riviera has become a legendary vacation locale for the rich and famous. First, it was a charming fisherman's retreat, then it became a star magnet in the late 1950s. From St. Tropez to Monaco, fishing boats had to make space for super yachts. Nonetheless, the Côte d'Azur style retains its rustic sheath. I've always admired the casual elegance of French women. I've travelled to the South of France many times and have always drawn inspiration from old films starring Bridgette Bardot, Jane Birkin, and Grace Kelly. Think flowy dresses, white linen, wide-brimmed hats, backless jumpsuits, and espadrilles. Here's what to consider when packing for the French Riviera.

Climate

The French Riviera enjoys a Mediterranean climate with mild winters and hot summers. Summers are warm, with temperatures ranging between 25-30°C (77-86°F). Winters are mild, with temperatures averaging around 10-15°C (50-59°F). When travelling in the summer, choose garments from natural fabrics such as linen, cotton, and lightweight silk. In winter, layer with wool and cashmere.

Culture

The French Riviera, or the Côte d'Azur, is renowned for its glamorous lifestyle. During the day, you can enjoy the laid-back style and channel your inner libertine with light, figure-hugging dresses or Breton striped jumpsuits and co-ord sets. In the evening, opt for classic elegance. Think white jumpsuits, silk slips, and cocktail dresses. Leave your distressed denim and slogan T-shirts at home.

Comfort

Much of the South of France is paved with cobblestone streets. Comfortable flat sandals or leather slides are a must. If you want to wear heels during the day, opt for a small block heel or wedges. In the evening, slip on a pair of elegant espadrilles or heels. Bring a large basket bag that doubles as a chic beach tote and a daytime bag, which holds your essentials and yummy finds at the local market. When visiting in winter, wear a pair of ballerina flats, leather sneakers, or ankle boots.

Colour scheme

Quintessential French Riviera style is anything white. Not only does it reflect the sun and keep you cool, but it also complements

French Riviera

your new Mediterranean tan! Win-win! Other classic and sophisticated colours like navy blue and creme are popular. If you want to be more playful, select outfits in pastel shades such as canary, lime, butterscotch, holland tulip, or blush. Experiment with floral prints, Breton stripes, and nautical designs.

Textures

Choose fabrics like chiffon, silk, or linen to keep fresh and comfortable. Stay cosy with natural fabrics such as wool and cashmere and introduce a bit of cool-girl attitude with a leather jacket. Add a straw bag from any natural woven material like raffia, straw, jute, and rattan to compliment your look. Accessorise with natural stones, seashells, beads, and large-chain jewellery. When in the South of France, I adore my silk Hermes scarf and love experimenting with it, whether tying it into a backless halter top or using it as a fabulous hair tie.

Must-haves

Essential items for the French Riviera include:

Clothing

- Lightweight dresses
- Lightweight tops
- Lightweight trousers
- Shorts
- Skirt
- Jumpsuit

French Riviera

- Swimming suit(s)

- Cover up(s)

- Cardigan or shawl for chilly evenings

- Light jacket or blazer (autumn and spring)

- Warm jacket (winter)

- Leather sneakers or ankle boots (autumn, spring, winter)

Footwear

- Sandals

- Espadrilles

Accessories

- Wide-brimmed hat

- Straw bag

- Clutch for evening outfits

- Sunglasses

French Riviera

Good to have

A bright silk scarf can be used as a cover-up, headwear, or a top! Another style tip is bright lipstick in shades of red or coral, which can instantly elevate your look with minimal effort. *C'est très chic!*

Traditional fashion elements to consider

The Cote d'Azur has a rich and timeless style. This style is so popular that it has become a staple in our wardrobes. Incorporate nautical-inspired stripes, flowy dresses, tailored separates, and classic accessories like espadrilles or boat shoes to embrace the region's coastal chic aesthetic. Check out the French Riviera Collection on Pinterest for inspiration. Search for @travelwithstylecollection in the home search bar to find our curated boards.

French Riviera

NOTES

The Greek Islands

The Greek islands are known for their sunny weather, stunning beaches, and picturesque villages. Each island has its own charm, but all share iconic, white-washed towns, stunning Aegean blue waters, and a casual bohemian vibe, which make for a few common rules to follow when packing your vacation capsule. The natural palette of the Greek islands is bright and vivid, with deep blues, crisp whites, and warm yellows and oranges. Here's what to know when packing for the Greek islands.

Climate

The Greek Islands have a Mediterranean climate, characterized by hot, dry summers and mild, wet winters. Summers are sunny and hot, with temperatures ranging between 25-35°C (77-95°F). Winters are mild, with temperatures averaging around 10-15°C (50-59°F).

Ensure you have lightweight and breathable clothing suitable for the warm weather, along with a light cardigan or shawl for cooler evenings. Bring a warm jacket, sweater, and jeans during the winter months. Some islands, like Mykonos, are known for their strong winds. You shouldn't underestimate them. The first time I visited over Easter break, I was surprised by the powerful gusts, which blew at speeds over 30 km per hour. My hair was in complete disarray, and I felt chilled to the bone. To avoid a hair disaster and potential Marilyn Monroe subway scene moments, be sure to pack a cap or scarf to keep your locks in check and steer clear of floaty mini-skirts and dresses.

Culture

The Greek Islands have a rich cultural heritage deeply rooted in ancient history and mythology. The locals embrace a relaxed and laid-back lifestyle, emphasizing hospitality and enjoying life's pleasures. The Greeks love festivals, music, dancing, and showing off their beautiful bodies. The Greek Islands are not a place for modesty. Feel free to bring clothing that shows off your newly tanned arms, back, and legs. Of course, if you visit a Monastery, make sure that you wear a long dress or skirt and a pashmina that covers your shoulders and legs.

Comfort

Opt for lightweight, loose-fitting clothing that allows your skin to breathe in the sweltering heat. It can be challenging to get taxis, and most roads and paths are cobblestone, so you'll need shoes that

The Greek Islands

are easy to walk in. Pack a pair of flat sandals or espadrilles for the day and a pair of wedges for the evening. Ensure that the wedges are comfortable and provide proper support for your ankle, as the terrain can be uneven.

Colour scheme

Embrace a colour palette inspired by the stunning island land-scapes, such as shades of blue reflecting the crystal-clear waters, crisp white representing the traditional Cycladic architecture, and pops of bright colours reminiscent of the gorgeous bougainvillea and sunsets. White and blue stripes work perfectly in this coastal environment and mix well with most other colours. All-white-everything looks will also pop against those magical sunsets. Bold orange and fuchsia will contrast beautifully with the blue domes and white-washed walls.

Textures

Embrace light and airy textures that suit the island's atmosphere. Linen is the perfect material for Greece since it's breezy and keeps you from sweating. Incorporate textures such as crochet, lace, or embroidered details to add a touch of bohemian charm to your outfits.

Must-haves

Essential items for the Greek Islands include:

The Greek Islands

Clothing

- Lightweight dress
- Linen/ cotton shorts or skirts
- Wide linen trousers
- Breathable tops and blouses
- Swimsuit(s)
- Cover up(s)
- Light cardigan or pashmina for cooler evenings
- Elegant dress for the evenings
- Long-sleeve tops (spring, autumn, winter)
- Jeans (spring, autumn, winter)
- Sweater (early spring, late autumn and winter)
- Medium to heavy jacket (winter)

Footwear

- Sandals or espadrilles
- Flip-flops
- Comfortable sneakers for exploring archaeological sites

Accessories

- Wide-brimmed hat
- Cross-body bag
- Straw beach bag

The Greek Islands

- Light scarf for protection against the wind
- Sunglasses
- Warm scarf and gloves (winter)

Good to have

Because it is scorching during the day, a reusable water bottle and a fan come in handy while exploring the town. Also, pack plenty of sunscreens and insect repellent.

Traditional fashion elements to consider

The Greek Islands have a distinct style to inspire your outfits. Think Greek Goddess with flowy maxi dresses, off-the-shoulder tops, or skirts with colourful patterns inspired by ancient Greek motifs. Embrace the simplicity of Grecian-inspired draping and asymmetrical silhouettes. Complete your look with gold accessories and delicate jewellery featuring Greek-inspired symbols like the evil eye or the key of life. Also, consider Greek-inspired leather sandals with metallic elements and woven straw bags. You will be able to pick some up at the local shops if you don't own any. Check out the Greek Islands Collection on Pinterest for inspiration. Search for @ travelwithstylecollection in the home search bar to find our curated boards.

The Greek Islands

NOTES

The Greek Islands

Hong Kong

ong Kong is a magical place. An intersection of the Eastern and Western cultures and a centre of commerce for the entire world. It has moved hands many times throughout history. Hong Kong is known for its bustling street markets, awe-inspiring skyline, delectable food, and iconic cultural festivals. It is also one of the most cosmopolitan and high-tech cities in Asia. Both locals and expats have a high benchmark for clothing choices.

Climate

Summers are hot and rainy, with temperatures ranging from 25-33°C (77-91°F) and humidity between 80% and 90%. Monsoon season is June, July, and August. Pack lightweight, breathable clothing and layer up with light cardigans or pashmina indoors. Remember to bring a raincoat or a shell jacket.

Winters are mild and drier, with temperatures averaging 15-20°C (59-68°F) and humidity at 72%. It is cooler from mid-December to mid-February, so bring your warmer layers. Leave your flip-flops, short dresses, and strappy tops at home in favour of long-sleeved tops, sweaters, trousers, and a light jacket. While these temperatures may not seem too cold, the high humidity amplifies the cold. Also, the buildings in Hong Kong aren't built to retain heat, so include warm pyjamas and socks to wear back at your hotel or apartment. During my visit to Hong Kong, I stayed with a friend who kindly warned me about this aspect of the weather during the winter months. I came well-prepared. Hong Kong is one of those destinations where the chilly weather can sneak up on you. So, I'm glad to pass on this travel wisdom to you!

In Spring, the weather is unstable, with the average temperature at 23°C/73°F and humidity at 82%. In autumn, the best time to visit Hong Kong, the weather is warm and pleasant with clear, sunny days. The average temperature is around 23°C/73°F with humidity at 72%.

Culture

Because Hong Kong is a vibrant fusion of Eastern and Western cultures, the heritage is influenced by both Chinese traditions and British colonial history. It is a fashion and designer-conscious city, particularly among young people. Hong Kong is a great place to bring your designer clothes and accessories.

Generally, older Hong Kongese dress modestly. However, the younger generation is less conservative. In summer's full heat and humidity, you will see plenty of camisoles, T-shirts, and shorts. As a

Hong Kong

rule of thumb, dress in a smart, casual style to fit in. However, dress modestly when visiting temples and local cultural sites. It's worth noting that some restaurants may only accept entry if you're well-dressed. So, you may want to change before heading out to dinner. If bringing a swimsuit, go for a one-piece over a bikini.

If you are in Hong Kong on business, formal suits are the norm for both men and women. If you're a woman doing business in Hong Kong, consider wearing a suit by a recognized label. The locals believe that successful people should invest in high-quality clothing and be well-dressed and polished. Wear flats or a low heel and accessorize with jade jewellery or a designer bag.

Comfort

Opt for lightweight and breathable clothing made from natural fabrics like cotton or linen, which you can layer as the weather changes throughout the day. Choose comfortable, water-resistant shoes for walking long distances. It's a good idea to bring several pairs of trainers or slip-on flats, which you can swap out if necessary. Also, pack a light sweater or pashmina, as the air-conditioning can be harsh. Finally, consider including warm loungewear to slip into at your hotel or Airbnb, as it can be chilly indoors during winter.

Colour scheme

The locals tend to dress conservatively in style and colour, favouring black, white, navy, and grey tones. Young Hong Kongese tend to dress with a touch of quirkiness and a pop of colour. Create a mix of bold and neutral tones, such as browns, blues, blacks, and greys,

Hong Kong

with pops of yellow, orange, green, or red. Avoid whites and nude colours because they can become see-through in the rain!

Textures

Choose fabrics that offer comfort and versatility in Hong Kong's climate. Lightweight and breathable materials like cotton, linen, viscose, and silk work all year round. Embrace textures like chiffon, lace, or mesh for a touch of elegance for the evening outfits. Layer with knits and oversized cardigans during chilly winter months.

Must-haves

Essential items for Hong Kong include:

Winter

Clothing
▪ Long trousers or jeans
▪ Long-sleeve shirts and blouses
▪ Elegant blouse
▪ Warm, tailored trousers
▪ Warm, knitted dress
▪ Sweater or knit cardigan
▪ Warm jacket or coat

Hong Kong

Footwear

- Comfortable, water-resistant sneakers
- Water-resistant boots
- Pair of smart shoes for restaurants

Accessories

- Sunglasses
- Crossbody bag or backpack
- Clutch for evenings out
- Pashmina
- Umbrella

Summer

Clothing

- Lightweight dress
- Lightweight, breathable tops
- Lightweight trousers
- Evening dress
- Shorts and skirts
- Swimwear and cover-up
- Cardigan or shawl for indoor spaces

Footwear

- Comfortable sandals
- Comfortable sneakers
- Dress shoes for evenings out

Accessories

- Sunhat or cap
- Sunglasses
- Crossbody bag or backpack
- Clutch for evenings out
- Pashmina
- Umbrella
- Waterproof bag or clutch for electronics

Spring and Autumn:

Clothing

- Long trousers or jeans
- Shirts, t-shirts and blouses
- Raincoat or poncho
- Skirt
- Casual day-time dress
- Evening dress or pantsuit

Hong Kong

- Light jacket
- Sweaters or cardigans

Footwear

- Comfortable, waterproof shoes
- Dress shoes for evenings out

Accessories

- Sunhat or cap
- Sunglasses
- Crossbody bag or backpack
- Clutch for evenings out
- Pashmina
- Umbrella

Hong Kong

Good to have

It's helpful to have a fan in the sweltering heat, a compact travel umbrella for unexpected rain showers, and a small travel-sized toiletry kit for freshening up on the go. If you don't have a compact umbrella, you can easily buy an inexpensive, decent one there. Consider packing some workout gear like biker shorts or leggings for exploring the city's forests or Hong Kong's hiking trails. Finally, consider investing in some athletic chafe guards to spare your inner thighs from the humidity.

Traditional fashion elements to consider

While Hong Kong is a modern and cosmopolitan city, you can draw inspiration from traditional Chinese fashion elements. Consider incorporating elements like Mandarin collars, *qipao* dresses, or *cheongsam*-inspired blouses. Embrace elegant and tailored garments with sleek silhouettes. Accessorise with traditional-inspired jewellery, such as jade or pearl pieces. Jade is believed to carry the energy of luck, wisdom, and good fortune. If you don't own a piece of jade jewellery, be sure to pick one up at the local stores in the Jade Market in Kowloon. For inspiration on what to wear, check out the Hong Kong Collection on Pinterest. Search for @travelwithstylecollection in the home search bar to find our curated boards.

Hong Kong

NOTES

Istanbul

Once the heart of the Byzantine Empire during its days as Constantinople, Istanbul is now the beating heart of modern Turkey. Istanbul is a cosmopolitan and secular city with a penchant for creativity and self-expression. It is world-renowned for its iconic landmarks like the Hagia Sophia and the Blue Mosque, Turkish hospitality, flavourful cuisine, and bustling bazaars. In general, Istanbulite women dress stylishly, adhering to Western fashion trends and expressing their own unique street style. This isn't the place to look sloppy in your leggings and oversized T-shirt. Also, the locals tend to dress up at night, so make sure you have a few looks ready for the evening. Finally, Istanbul offers excellent shopping. Whether you want handmade leather goods, international brands, or home-grown designers, there are plenty of choices for every taste and budget. Pack lightly, as you will likely add items to your luggage on your return flight.

Climate

Istanbul experiences a moderate Mediterranean climate with distinct seasons. Summers are hot and dry, with temperatures averaging around 25-30°C (77-86°F). During August, the temperatures climb to the high 30°C (95°F), so be prepared for some serious heat. Pack light and breathable fabrics, oversized shirts or kaftans, loose and effortless dresses, and sunhat and sunglasses for sun protection.

Winters are cold and wet, with temperatures ranging from 5-15°C (41-59°F). It gets colder than you'd expect. January often brings snow. Pack warm trousers, sweaters, a warm, water-resistant coat, or jacket, and don't forget a woolly hat, gloves, and scarf. When I travelled to celebrate New Year's Eve in Istanbul, I brought my mother's vintage fur coat. It was definitely weather-appropriate, keeping me warm and snug, despite the freezing temperatures at night. If you do not experience such harsh winters back home and don't own such clothing, don't worry. You can always buy great winter jackets and accessories in Istanbul. Finally, you will need stable and warm footwear, such as boots with a warm lining paired with warm socks.

Spring and autumn offer mild and pleasant weather, with temperatures ranging from 10-25°C (50-77°F), making it ideal for walking and enjoying the city. Packing a few cardigans, sweaters, and a jacket will suffice.

Culture

Turkey is a Muslim-majority country, and Istanbul is a Muslim-majority city. You'll see some Turkish women wearing varying

Istanbul

degrees of *hijab* (cover). Some women will be fully covered, some partially covered with a headscarf, but many will be in short shorts, mini dresses, and camisoles. While there's no restriction on what you can wear, but you will be more comfortable erring on the side of modesty. Wearing revealing clothing can attract unwanted attention. As a rule of thumb, wear midi or maxi skirts or dresses, avoid cleavage, and cover your stomach. A strict dress code must be followed when visiting religious sites. At mosques, wear clothes that cover your shoulders and knees and cover your head with a scarf.

Comfort

Comfort is essential when exploring Istanbul's vibrant neighbour-hoods and historical sites. Pack your comfortable walking shoes (make sure they are well-broken before the trip). Depending on the season, this can be flat mules, leather sneakers, boots, or sandals with a low block heel that is suitable for uneven terrain and cobble-stone streets. Avoid wearing a lot of flashy jewellery in places like the Grand Bazaar, Blue Mosque areas, and Taksim-Istiklal to avoid becoming a target of petty theft. Avoid carrying a big handbag with all your belongings. Instead, bring a small-cross body or messenger bag to keep your essentials in sight when visiting busy, tourist areas.

Istanbul

Colour scheme

Black is a popular clothing choice for locals, but you should incor-porate some colour to break up your neutrals. The city is full of beautiful colours and patterns in the markets, tiles, and rugs, so reflect these in your travel capsule. Embrace earthy tones like warm browns, terracotta, and olive greens to reflect the city's historic architecture and natural surroundings. Combine them with vibrant hues like turquoise or deep blues reminiscent of the Bosphorus and the city's mesmerising tiles.

Textures

During the hot summer, focus on lightweight fabrics like cotton, viscose, and linen. Experiment with textures like lace, embroidery, or woven details inspired by Turkish craftsmanship. Layer with a light cardigan, scarf, or denim jacket in the evenings. Opt for warm fabrics such as wool, cashmere, and thermal blends in winter.

Must-haves

Essential items for Istanbul will vary depending on the season:

Summer

Clothing
■ Lightweight midi or maxi dress
■ Lightweight, loose trousers
■ Breathable tops and blouses
■ Lightweight midi skirt
■ Light cardigan or denim jacket
■ Swimwear and cover-up

Istanbul

Footwear

- Comfortable sandals
- Leather slides or mules
- Dress shoes for evenings out

Accessories

- Shawl
- Sunhat
- Sunglasses
- Cross-body or messenger bag

Winter

Clothing

- Warm winter jacket or coat
- Warm socks
- Thermal layers
- Long-sleeved tops and shirts
- Warm sweaters
- Knitted dress
- Warm trousers

Istanbul

Footwear

- Warm, waterproof boots
- Dress shoes for evenings out

Accessories

- Warm scarf
- Warm hat
- Gloves or mittens
- Crossbody or messenger bag

Spring / Autumn

Clothing

- Jeans or trousers
- Long-sleeve tops and shirts
- Casual, long-sleeve dresses
- Elegant blouse
- Elegant dress or pantsuit
- Cardigans or sweaters
- Rainproof jacket or trench coat
- Medium-weight jacket (early spring and late autumn)

Footwear

- Comfortable, water-resistant boots

Istanbul

- Comfortable sneakers
- Dress shoes for evenings out

Accessories

- Scarf
- Crossbody or messenger bag
- Sunglasses

Good to have

A travel-sized umbrella is helpful for unexpected rain. During the summer, consider packing a small fan and anti-chafing patches. During the winter, consider bringing thermal tops and leggings.

Traditional fashion elements to consider

Consider incorporating traditional elements of Turkish fashion, such as a kaftan or harem pants as a nod to the Turkish *salvar*. Also, consider flat mules inspired by traditional Turkish slippers into your outfits. Embrace the prints and patterns inspired by Turkish textiles. Accessorise with traditional jewellery like statement earrings or try a bejewelled headband to elevate your hairstyle and give it an oriental look. For inspiration on what to wear in Istanbul, check out our Istanbul Collection on Pinterest. Search for @travelwithstylecollection in the home search bar to find our curated boards.

Istanbul

NOTES

Istanbul

London

lthough London is known for many things, a fashion-for-ward capital is not one of them. Nonetheless, there is undoubtedly a London look. Having spent five years living there, I'm here to break it down for you. When considering how to dress, remember that London is a city of contrasts and juxta-positions. On the one hand, it's all about embracing the eclectic, unique, and eccentric. On the other hand, Londoners tend to dress in the classic style, preferring neutral colours and tailored silhou-ettes. The city style is tailored and conservative with an edge. So, avoid items such as UGG boots, Crocs, and sweatpants.

The weather plays a huge role in what to wear in London. Not only do the seasons affect your choice of clothing, but the time of day also plays a role. There is a lot of variation in the weather on a typical day. So, layers are always a good idea. Here's what to know when packing for London.

Climate

London experiences a temperate maritime climate characterized by mild winters and mild summers. The average temperature in winter ranges from 2-8°C (36-46°F), while summer temperatures hover around 18-25°C (64-77°F). Rainfall is common throughout the year, so bring a trench coat and an umbrella. There's one thing you need to be prepared for: British weather is unpredictable. Sunny mornings often end with rain, and cloudy days turn into balmy evenings. Always, always, always check the weather forecast before your trip.

Culture

London is a melting pot of diverse cultures, which makes it fertile soil for an eclectic art, music, and culture scene. London keeps a firm grip on its history and origins, which is evident in the way the locals dress. Most locals favour a tailored and sophisticated look, which features a button-down shirt, trousers, and a tailored blazer or coat.

At the same time, Londoners can be incredibly diverse and eccentric in their style, dressing head to toe in goth, punk, or retro. There's also a penchant for academic style, with argyle vests, blazers, pleated skirts, brogues, and loafers. Feel free to incorporate grunge, the uni aesthetic, or retro elements into your looks.

Curiously, London style may differ from postcode to postcode. For example, Chelsea residents are fond of colourful chinos, espadrilles, and skinny jeans with riding boots. While I lived there, Sunday strolls down King's Road in the spring were synonymous with wearing dark blue skinny jeans, a colourful sweater, boots, and a classic trench coat.

London

Meanwhile, North and East London residents prefer black skinny jeans, Converse, and punk-inspired looks. With my Chelsea style, I always stood out when visiting my friends in Angel.

Comfort

Opt for comfortable and water-resistant footwear, such as boots or loafers. You'll be walking a lot. If you're traveling in the summer, take a pair of comfortable leather sandals in case you get lucky and catch the beautiful sunny days. When assembling your looks, remember that it needs to have at least two layers in summer and three or four layers in winter, including thermal undergarments. Pack a rain jacket or trench coat, a compact umbrella, and a cardigan for exploring the city during the day.

Colour scheme

Londoners love neutral colours such as navy, grey, black, white, and beige. It's an excellent opportunity to assemble monochromatic looks and experiment with textures as you layer. If you want to add colour to your outfits, adhere to the "No more than three colours" rule. But if you feel like dressing up head-to-toe in fuchsia or lime green, London is a great place to do so, especially if you go to a festival or an artsy meetup. Avoid flashy colours when visiting high-end establishments, museums, theatres, or business meetings. When it comes to prints, opt for classic prints such as graphics and florals. Pair a floral dress or blouse with a more tailored element such as a blazer for contrast.

London

Textures

Experiment with fabrics and materials to add more depth and interest to your looks. Mix cosy wool blends with leather in winter and throw on a leather or denim jacket over a linen dress in the summer. Play with textures to create truly unique looks that showcase your personality and style.

Must-haves

Here's a list of must-have items for your London trip:

Summer

Clothing
▪ T-shirts, tops, and sleeveless blouses
▪ White button-down shirt
▪ Jeans or trousers
▪ Skirt
▪ Lightweight, midi or maxi dress
▪ Evening dress
▪ Cardigan
▪ Denim jacket or blazer
▪ Trench coat or parka

London

Footwear

- Comfortable shoes such as ballet flats or sandals
- Comfortable sneakers
- Dress shoes for evenings out

Accessories

- Compact umbrella
- Cross-body or messenger bag
- Heels for evenings out
- Clutch for evenings out

Spring and Autumn

Clothing

- T-shirts, tops, and blouses
- White button-down shirt
- Jeans or trousers
- Skirt
- Casual dress
- Evening dress
- Cardigan or sweater
- Turtleneck
- Leather jacket
- Trench coat or parka

London

Footwear

- Comfortable shoes such as boots, loafers, or converse
- Comfortable sneakers
- Dress shoes for evenings out

Accessories

- Compact umbrella
- Cross-body or messenger bag
- Lightweight scarf
- Clutch for evenings out

Winter

Clothing

- White button-down shirt
- Long-sleeve tops
- Blouse
- Thermal undergarments
- Jumpers and sweaters
- Jeans
- Warm, tailored trousers
- Skirt

London

- Warm coat
- Turtleneck
- Woollen blazer

Footwear

- Warm, waterproof boots
- Comfortable sneakers
- Dress shoes for evenings out

Accessories

- Compact umbrella
- Warm scarf
- Gloves or mittens
- Warm hat
- Crossbody or messenger bag
- Clutch for evenings out

London

Good to have

When travelling in winter, bring some thermal leggings, which you can wear under your trousers or dress. Also, consider packing a fleece or down vest as an extra layer for those frigid winter days. Finally, grab a lip balm to protect your lips against cold, dry air.

Traditional fashion elements to consider

Great Britain offers many stylistic elements that blend well with contemporary style. To fit in with the Londoners, consider incorporating a knitted vest, garments made of tweed, a scarf or top with plaid patterns, punk rock studs, quilted gilets, and jackets à la Barbour. For inspiration on what to wear in London, check out our London Collection on Pinterest. Search for @travelwithstylecollection in the home search bar to find our curated boards.

London

NOTES

_____

_____

_____

_____

_____

_____

_____

_____

_____

_____

_____

_____

_____

London

Marrakech

arrakech is a city steeped in rich history and vibrant culture known for its bustling souks, stunning architecture, traditional music, and flavourful cuisine. To enjoy its rich culture and flavours best, ensure you have appropriate clothes that respect local customs and fit the seasonal weather. The dress code in Marrakech is similar to parts of the Middle East. Here's what to note when packing for Marrakech.

Climate

Marrakech experiences a hot, semi-arid climate characterized by scorching summers and mild winters. During summer, temperatures can soar above 40°C (104°F), while winter temperatures range from 8-20°C (46-68°F). It gets very chilly at night during the winter months, so bring sweaters, a warm jacket, and warm pyjamas. From September to April, rain is likely, so be sure to pack a raincoat, an umbrella, and waterproof shoes.

Culture

Respect for the country's culture affects what to wear in Marrakech. Islam is the main religion in Morocco, so the local women of Marrakech dress modestly. Some will wear more Western clothing, while others will wear the traditional *djellaba*, abaya, and headscarf. Female tourists are not required to cover their heads. However, you may be asked to wear a headdress when visiting religious sites. So, ensure you have a light pashmina, which can double as a shawl and headdress when needed.

When packing for Marrakech, leave your short shorts and camisoles at home. You want to bring items that cover your knees and shoulders. If you want to wear jeans, it's a good idea to wear an oversized shirt or a tunic-style top to cover your curves. Avoid crop tops, backless tops, figure-hugging dresses, low-cut tops, and anything that exposes cleavage, too much skin, or is figure-hugging. Finally, avoid anything made of sheer fabric. If you can see your underwear through it, leave it at home.

Comfort

Opt for loose, breathable clothing from natural fibres like cotton or linen. Lightweight and flowy dresses, loose linen trousers, and airy tops are ideal for staying cool and comfortable in the Moroccan heat. Remember to wear comfortable, closed-toe shoes for walking. The streets in Medina are often wet and messy, and the cobbled streets are pretty ragged. Espadrilles, mules, ankle boots, and leather trainers will work well. Finally, limit displays of flashy jewellery or luxury handbags to avoid unwanted attention.

Marrakech

Colour scheme

Marrakech is known for its vibrant prints and colour palette. Embrace the city's spirit by integrating rich, bold hues into your travel capsule. Think vibrant oranges, deep blues, earthy reds, and golden yellows. Feel free to mix and match colours to create eye-catching and stylish looks.

Textures

Marrakech is renowned for its intricate textiles and traditional craftsmanship. Incorporate textures such as embroidered details, woven fabrics, and embellishments like sequins or beads into your outfits. Embrace the beauty of Moroccan textiles and pay homage to the artistry through an inspired statement piece. Ensure you have cosy knitted sweaters and a warm waterproof jacket if you travel in winter, as temperatures drop significantly.

Must-haves

When travelling to Marrakech, make sure to pack:

Summary

Clothing
▪ Lightweight and loose trousers
▪ Lightweight tops and blouses
▪ Midi skirt

Marrakech

- Maxi dress
- Oversize shirt
- Swimwear and cover-up

Footwear

- Comfortable closed-toe shoes
- Sturdy sandals

Accessories

- Wide-brimmed hat
- Crossbody bag or tote
- Light shawl or scarf
- Sunglasses

Winter

Clothing

- Warm trousers or jeans
- Long-sleeve tops and shirts
- T-shirts for layering
- Warm sweaters
- Warm jacket
- Warm socks

Marrakech

Footwear

- Warm, closed toe shoes
- Comfortable, waterproof boots

Accessories

- Sunglasses
- Crossbody bag or backpack

Spring / Autumn

Clothing

- Long trousers
- Long-sleeve tops and blouses
- T-shirts for layering
- Midi skirt
- Maxi dress
- Cardigans or sweaters
- Light jacket

Footwear

- Comfortable walking shoes
- Comfortable, waterproof shoes

Marrakech

Accessories

- Wide-brimmed hat
- Sunglasses
- Pashmina
- Crossbody bag or tote

Good to have

If your hotel has a pool, be sure to bring a swimsuit and a kaftan or cover-up. Also, if you plan to make a trip to the desert, remember to pack warm layers, such as a hoodie or thermals, as the desert gets chilly at night.

Traditional fashion elements to consider

Moroccan fashion is known for its intricate details, vibrant patterns, and flowing silhouettes. Consider incorporating elements such as kaftans, *djellabas*, *balgha* shoes, and traditional prints into your capsule. *Sarouel*, a loose-fitting cotton trouser with an elastic waist and cuffs, can also be a great alternative to jeans. Finally, add accessories like intricate statement jewellery, woven belts, embellished slippers, and clutches to complete your Moroccan-inspired look. For inspiration on what to wear, check out our Marrakech Collection on Pinterest. Search for @travelwithstylecollection in the home search bar to find our curated boards.

Marrakech

NOTES

_____

_____

_____

_____

_____

_____

_____

_____

_____

_____

_____

_____

_____

_____

_____

_____

Marrakech

Paris

aris is a city designed to explore and wander. Your days will likely turn into nights, so it's essential to wear outfits that can take you from museums to evening aperitif and from shopping to dinner.

The quintessential French outfit is suitable for any time or place. It is made up of timeless classics: a good-quality blazer, a simple dress, classic jeans, smart, comfortable shoes, and minimal jewellery. The key to dressing like *une vraie parisienne* is simplicity. Forget loud prints, the overwhelming presence of logos, or an abundance of embellishments and accessories. Here's what to know when packing for Paris.

Climate

Paris has a temperate maritime climate, with mild summers and cold winters. Summer temperatures range from 20-25°C (68-77°F), while winter temperatures can drop to 3-6°C (37-43°F). Think airy cotton and linen dresses during the summer, paired with light cardigans or a trench coat in the evenings. Blazers, cute knits, and leather jackets during the shoulder seasons. Warm, chunky sweaters and cosy scarves during the wintertime. During my work trips to Paris in winter, my go-to outfit consisted of tailored black trousers, a cashmere turtleneck, a long black coat, ankle boots with a slight heel, a classic shoulder bag, leather gloves, and a woollen fedora. This simple look transitioned seamlessly from the office to after-work walks along the Seine and dinners with friends.

Culture

Parisians are known for their elegant and sophisticated approach to dressing, valuing quality over quantity. Less is more, so go for minimalist and timeless looks. Parisians prioritize fit and material, ensuring their clothes enhance natural beauty and flatter their silhouette. When it comes to accessorizing, choose one accessory to upgrade your outfit instead of layering your jewellery. Parisians don't appreciate in-your-face displays of wealth and ostentatious-ness. However, you may incorporate one statement piece (such as chunky earrings, a show-stopping necklace, or a statement brooch) to add a touch of individuality to your look.

Comfort

Comfort is key in Paris, where you'll likely be doing a lot of walking and exploring. Opt for chic yet comfortable clothing, such as well-fitted jeans, breathable, simple tops, and a classic trench coat.

Paris

Alternatively, wear a slip-on dress and pair it with ankle boots for a casual daytime outfit. In the evening, you can swap the boots for chic mules and add polished jewellery for a more elegant look. Layering is essential. Bring a lightweight sweater or cardigan to wear as needed. While Paris is a fashion capital, it is also a city full of cobblestone streets. High heels during the day will not only make it difficult to walk distances, but you will likely end up with scuffed heels. Instead, opt for a comfortable pair of ballet flats, ankle boots, or loafers. Remember that your shoes need to be *really* comfortable and preferably waterproof.

Colour scheme

Parisians dress in an understated and elegant colour palette. While you may love the *Emily in Paris* TV show wardrobe, stick to classic and neutral colours like black, white, navy, beige, and grey in your travel capsule. These colours are easy to mix and match and exude a sense of effortless sophistication. If you must add colour to your looks, opt for pastels and muted tones such as moss green, burgundy red, and ochre.

Textures

Choose natural fabrics that will be breathable: cotton, linen, and rayon in the summer; wool and cashmere in the winter. If you'd like to add a touch of luxury, consider bringing silk blouses, silk slip dresses, cashmere sweaters, leather trousers, and a velvet blazer. Depending on the time of year you're visiting, consider taking a silk or cashmere scarf to accessorize with. I recommend that you avoid

Paris

wearing suede jackets or shoes because there is almost always a high chance of rain.

Must-haves

Some essential items for your trip to Paris:

Spring

Clothing

- Multifunctional dress to dress up and down
- Smart pair of jeans (solid colour, no rips)
- Elegant top or blouse
- Cardigan or light sweater
- Plain white T-shirt or shirt
- Oversized blazer
- Slip dress
- Trench coat

Footwear

- Ankle boots, ballet flats or loafers
- Pair of chic mules or pumps (evenings)

Accessories

- Scarf
- Crossbody bag

Paris

- Elegant jewellery
- Sunglasses

Summer

Clothing

- Multifunctional dress to dress up and down
- Smart pair of jeans (solid colour, no rips)
- Elegant top or blouse
- Cardigan or light sweater
- Plain white T-shirt or shirt
- Oversized blazer
- Slip dress
- Trench coat

Footwear

- White sneakers or ballet flats
- Espadrilles or sandals
- Pair of chic mules or pumps (evenings)

Accessories

- Silk scarf
- Crossbody bag
- Basket bag

Paris

- Elegant jewellery
- Sunhat
- Sunglasses

Autumn

Clothing

- Multifunctional dress to dress up and down
- Smart pair of jeans (solid colour, no rips)
- Elegant top or blouse
- Plain white T-shirt or shirt
- Oversized blazer
- Slip dress
- Good quality knits
- Trench coat

Footwear

- Ankle boots or loafers
- Comfortable sneakers
- Pair of chic mules or pumps (evenings)

Accessories

- Warm scarf
- Crossbody bag

Paris

- Elegant jewellery
- Leather gloves and warm hat

Winter

Clothing

- Thermal tops and leggings
- Multifunctional dress to dress up and down
- Smart pair of jeans (solid colour, no rips)
- Elegant top or blouse
- Plain white T-shirt or shirt
- Oversized blazer
- Good quality knits
- Warm socks
- Warm overcoat

Footwear

- Warm waterproof boots
- Pair of chic mules or pumps (evenings)

Accessories

- Warm scarf
- Warm gloves or mittens
- Warm hat

Paris

- Crossbody bag
- Elegant jewellery

Good to have

If you're traveling in the summer, consider bringing along a sleek and elegant basket bag for a truly Parisian look. If you're traveling in the winter, bring a warm beret and a pair of leather gloves which will keep you warm and elegant. Paris can get much colder than what the weather app suggests, so it's good to be prepared. It's also a good idea to pack a compact umbrella.

Traditional fashion elements to consider

Parisian style is known for its classic and timeless pieces. Incorporate elements such as Breton stripes, vintage leather accessories from famous Parisian brands, and a large pair of sunglasses. A little black dress is a staple for evenings out. Pay attention to small details, such as accessorizing with delicate jewellery and opting for statement pieces that you can pick up at one of Paris' many shops and flea markets. Indeed, the French have a deep appreciation for vintage fashion. Vintage shops are scattered throughout the streets of Paris, offering a treasure trove of unique and timeless pieces. There you will find one-of-a-kind pieces, timeless accessories, and even designer items from bygone eras. It's a must-do activity for fashion enthusiasts visiting Paris! For inspiration on what to wear to Paris, check out our Paris Collection on Pinterest. Search for @travelwith-stylecollection in the home search bar to find our curated boards.

Paris

NOTES

Paris

Rome

Because Rome is Italy's governmental seat, the main financial centre, and the heart of the Italian movie industry, you may assume that Romans are always dressed to the nines. Yes, Italians like to dress up. But when creating your capsule for your trip to Rome, focus on smart, casual clothing. Consider well-fitting jeans, an elegant wrap dress, a statement skirt, a camel coat, and a crisp white shirt as your go-to. Wardrobes in Rome are bold but not over the top. One statement piece paired with a simple knit or a T-shirt and we're off to the races. Confidence is key, so bring along items that make you look and feel good! Here's what to consider when packing for Rome.

Climate

Rome experiences a Mediterranean climate with hot summers and chilly, humid winters. In the summer, temperatures can soar to

32°C (90°F) so lightweight and breathable clothing is essential. In the winter, daytime temperatures hover around 10°C to 15°C (50°F to 59°F). It gets very chilly, especially in the evenings, so you'll need layers and a warm coat. The autumn and spring temperatures range between 15°C to 24°C (59°F to 75°F). The weather can also vary greatly throughout the day, so come prepared with layers.

Culture

Italian people have an innate sense of class and style. The Romans appreciate well-tailored, elegant outfits. However, given the number of tourists the city welcomes, it's a hodgepodge of style. Locals appreciate dressing with sophistication, and you'll notice them wearing simple yet incredibly stylish and well-fitted outfits.

On your visit to Rome, you will most likely visit St Peter's Basilica and the Vatican City. Both have a strictly enforced dress code: everyone must cover their legs and shoulders. So, dress appropriately, or you will find yourself buying paper trousers! On my visit to the Vatican City, I wore a simple, cotton dress that fell just below my knees. I also brought a shawl to drape over my shoulders and arms. This outfit allowed me to show respect inside the Vatican while staying comfortable in the summer heat outdoors.

Rome

Comfort

Comfortable footwear is crucial when exploring Rome's cobblestone streets, fashionable cafes, and innumerable historic sites. If you're travelling in the summer, choose a pair of comfortable leather sandals. Make sure they provide cushioning and support for long walks. White leather trainers are also a popular and versatile option, which can easily be paired with jeans, skirts, and dresses. If you want a more polished look or are travelling in spring or fall, opt for a pair of leather loafers. If you're visiting in winter, ensure you have a pair of comfortable boots that can handle the wet cobblestone streets and keep you snug in the chill. Bring along a pair of elegant heels that can inject a dose of Italian sexiness into your evening looks. In the summer, choose a simple heeled sandal in a bright shade. If you're not a fan of heels, opt for a pair of wedges. In winter, a pair of leather pumps will do the trick.

Colour scheme

Embrace a sophisticated colour palette of neutrals such as whites, beiges, and blacks. They easily mix and match and fit in perfectly with the stunning architecture of Rome. Use accessories with pops of colour, like deep red or cobalt blue, to add zest to your look. If you feel like you need more colour in your life, use contrasting or complementary colours to impress or pair similar hues for a more subtle elegant look. If you're into prints, this is your place to shine. Include a few dresses and a blouse with bold prints, which you can wear both during the daytime and in the evenings.

Textures

For summertime, avoid fabrics like polyester and opt for breathable fabrics such as rayon, cotton, viscose, and linen. In winter, opt for wool, cashmere, wool blends, and leather.

Must-haves

Here are your must-haves for your trip to Rome.

Summer

Clothing

- Lightweight tops and T-shirts
- Wide linen or Capri trousers
- Statement skirt
- Lightweight and breathable dresses
- Light cardigan

Footwear

- Comfortable sandals
- Comfortable sneakers
- Dress shoes for evenings

Accessories

- Sunhat
- Sunglasses
- Lightweight shawl
- Shoulder bag or cross-body bag

Rome

Winter

Clothing

- Thermal tops
- Long-sleeve tops and shirts
- Blouse
- Sweaters
- Tailored jeans
- Warm trousers
- Statement skirt
- Knitted dress
- Warm socks
- Tights

Footwear

- Comfortable, waterproof boots
- Comfortable sneakers
- Dress shoes for evenings

Accessories

- Warm hat
- Gloves or mittens
- Warm scarf
- Shoulder bag or cross-body bag
- Sunglasses

Rome

Spring / Autumn

Clothing

- T-shirts for layering
- Long-sleeve shirts and blouses
- Statement skirt
- Casual dress
- Tailored jeans
- Cardigan or sweater
- Medium-weight jacket or trench coat

Footwear

- Comfortable walking shoes
- Waterproof boots
- Dress shoes for evenings

Accessories

- Sunglasses
- Shoulder bag or cross-body bag
- Scarf

Rome

Good to have

One other item you might consider is a classic suit to wear with sneakers and a T-shirt during the day, then elevate with a pair of heels and a silk blouse for an evening out.

An Italian saying goes, '*Marzo passerelle, esce il sole, prendi l'ombrello*'! It translates to crazy March, the sun comes, you take the umbrella! You never know when the heavens may open in Rome. A light, foldable umbrella or a light rain jacket could save you from getting completely drenched in a sudden shower.

Traditional fashion elements to consider

Embrace classic and timeless pieces like tailored blazers, suits, high-quality leather accessories, and well-fitted dresses. They all align with the Italian appreciation for elegance and style. If you're a fan of Italian designer brands, this is a great place to sport them. However, as with many tourist cities, pickpockets are rampant, so be wary of flaunting any valuables in overcrowded areas. For inspiration on what to wear to Rome, check out our Rome Collection on Pinterest. Search for @travelwithstylecollection in the home search bar to find our curated boards.

Rome

NOTES

_____

_____

_____

_____

_____

_____

_____

_____

_____

_____

_____

_____

_____

_____

Rome

Safari

When it comes to dressing for safari, there are three golden rules to follow. First of all, layering is your best friend. The second gold rule is colour. Stick to a neutral, earthy colour palette. The third is less is more. When you over-pack for a safari, it can become a burden. Aim to fit your capsule into a weekend or duffle bag and other essentials into a backpack. These recommendations apply to the typical game drive safari in a vehicle. If your holiday includes other activities like bush camping and gorilla trekking, consult with your tour operator to see if your itinerary requires any specific gear.

Climate

In most of Africa, seasons vary between wet and dry seasons. The dry season (June to October) in East Africa is hot. The rainy season (November to May) in East Africa brings mild, spring-like weather.

However, Southern Africa is the opposite. There the dry season (May to September) means chilly evenings and mornings. The rainy season in South Africa (October to April) can coincide with its hottest months.

It's essential to check the weather forecast and come prepared for mixed weather conditions by bringing layers. Although the savannah can be hot during the day, temperatures drop significantly at night. Also, remember that most game drives happen early in the morning or at dusk when it's the coldest. On the morning of our first safari in Kruger Park, I discovered my clothes weren't warm enough and had to improvise, layering my own clothes with my husband's. I pulled his warm tracksuit bottoms over my shorts and draped a blanket over my leather jacket to keep warm during the drive. As the day progressed and temperatures climbed, I gradually shed those layers, adapting to the changing conditions. I learned my lesson and always packed the necessary layers for my subsequent safari trips. Bring T-shirts, shorts, long-sleeve tops, long trousers, a sweater or fleece, a scarf, and a warm jacket. Pro tip: pack warm pyjamas as the lodges can get downright chilly at night. During that first safari experience, the night-time temperature inside the tent caught me off guard. Fortunately, our tent came with warm blankets and the staff provided us with hot water bottles to take to bed.

Safari

Culture

It is tempting to dress up in camo for a safari. However, it's illegal for civilians to wear camouflage in some African countries. Feel free to bring utility pants but avoid the camouflage print. Wear modest clothing if you're planning to visit local villages, covering your knees and shoulders. Also, avoid expensive or flashy jewellery.

Instead, embrace local craftsmanship and buy locally made earrings, bracelets, and necklaces to style your outfits.

Comfort

In addition to looking stylish for your social media, you want your safari outfits to protect you from the elements and insects. Comfort is key on a safari, as you'll spend much time outdoors and on safari drives. Opt for comfortable, mobile clothing that protects your skin. Safari jeeps are open. Some have a roof, while others don't. So, you'll be in the elements, whether it's the blazing African sun, a sudden rain shower, or the night chills.

As game drives begin in the early hours, wear multiple layers you can take off as the morning progresses. Wear a T-shirt or tank top as a base layer, a jumper, or a fleece zip up for warmth, and a jacket. A scarf does triple duty as an accessory, an extra layer, and a wrap over your face during a dusty drive.

Long trousers are a must as they protect your legs from scratches and mosquitos, a crucial feature in malaria regions. Opt for cargo or hiking pants, chinos, or khakis instead of jeans. I do not recommend jumpsuits or rompers on safari drives. You may need to relieve yourself in the bush. The last thing you want is to be entirely butt naked and look up to find a wild animal staring you down.

While you don't need walking boots, as you'll spend most of the time in a vehicle, you'll need comfy, breathable boots with a high top. Opt for a desert-style boot in canvas or leather. Also, bring long cotton socks to keep your feet dry and comfortable. Pack a wide-brimmed hat to keep the sun off your face. Since the equator goes right down the middle of Africa, expect intense UV rays. Try to get a hat with a string to keep it from flying off during drives.

Safari

Consider packing a cute co-ord set and flip-flops for lounging around your tent. Also, include a dress for a romantic dinner or sundowner. This can be a classic safari dress or a flowy maxi dress in a muted colour. Bring a shawl or cardigan, as the evenings get chilly. Finally, ensure you have a swimsuit if your camp has a pool.

Colour scheme

Neutral colours like khaki, brown, and tan are perfect during the dry season. Whereas browns and greens will help you match the vegetation in the rainy season. These colours will also help camouflage any dust or dirt on your safari adventure.

They say that blue and grey attract tsetse flies. Avoid black because it won't reflect the sun and keep you cool. Red or orange will stand out to the animals and scare them off, or worse, agitate them. Although, a loud jeep rumbling down the dirt road kicking up a cloud of sand with a load of tourists holding out massive cameras is likely more distracting to the wildlife than someone's crimson scarf. However, the colours are extra important for cycling or walking safaris, where you can get up close and personal with certain animals. Finally, if you are a fan of animal prints, this is your place to rock them!

Safari

Textures

You will want to keep your skin covered to protect it from the sun and insects. Opt for loose, breezy materials that don't stick to the skin. Lightweight and breathable natural fabrics like cotton, linen, and canvas, or technical synthetic blends are your go-to. They keep you ventilated in the heat and are easy to wash and dry.

Must-haves

Here is a list of essentials for an African Safari.

Clothing

- T-shirts and tank tops
- Long-sleeved shirt
- Long trousers
- Co-ord set for lounging
- Casual maxi dress
- Cardigan
- Fleece or jumper
- Warm, waterproof jacket
- Swimwear and cover-up (if your lodge has a pool)

Footwear

- Comfortable, breathable, and sturdy walking boots
- Waterproof hiking boots (wet season)
- Flip-flops or sandals for lounging

Safari

Accessories

- Backpack
- Wide-brimmed hat
- Scarf
- Warm gloves and hat for early morning game drives
- Sunglasses

Good to have

Bring mosquito repellent, a water bottle, and a portable charger for the game drives. Consider packing a waterproof bag or camera cover to protect your equipment during the rainy season. Ensure you pack a small medical kit with essentials like plasters, antihistamines, and painkillers.

Traditional fashion elements to consider

Depending on your safari destination, you may have a chance to visit local tribes or traditional markets. Here you can buy hand-made jewellery, traditional textiles, and accessories. In Kenya and Tanzania, the Maasai people are known for their vibrant traditional textiles, such as the *shuka* or Maasai blanket. Also, Maasai bead-work is an essential part of their culture, with intricately beaded jewellery and accessories like necklaces, bracelets, and earrings. In Botswana, the San people also have a rich tradition of beadwork. They create beautiful beadwork patterns on their clothing and

Safari

accessories, including necklaces, bracelets, and headbands. It's an excellent opportunity to support the local communities. However, it's important to remember that these traditional textiles and jewellery are a form of artistic expression and a way for these communities to showcase their cultural heritage and identity. They are often used in ceremonies, celebrations, and everyday life. When wearing traditional clothing, remember to do so authentically and respectfully. For inspiration on what to wear to a safari, check out our Safari Collection on Pinterest. Search for @travelwithstylecollection in the home search bar to find our curated boards.

Safari

Notes

_____

_____

_____

_____

_____

_____

_____

_____

_____

_____

_____

_____

_____

_____

_____

Safari

Singapore

ingapore stands out as a flourishing country that consists only of a small island city. In this unique city-state, you can experience the festival of lanterns, art, cocktails, wellness, luxury, and many local and multicultural events. Singapore boasts pristine nature, endless dining and entertainment, and many high-tech malls. There are a ton of opportunities for shopping and finding a bargain, so pack light if shopping is your favourite sport! Here's what to know when packing for Singapore.

Climate

Singapore has a tropical rainforest climate with consistently high temperatures and high humidity. The average temperature ranges from 25°C to 31°C (77°F to 88°F), and it is generally warm and humid, making lightweight, breathable, and moisture-wicking clothing essential.

With almost no seasonal variations, the two monsoon seasons are the only interruptions to the hot and sunny weather. The Northeast monsoon season lasts from December to March. The Southwest monsoon season lasts from June to September. Rainstorms are usually short but heavy, so take a compact umbrella. While it is hot outside, inside the air-conditioning will be blasting on high. Make sure to take a shawl, blazer, or cardigan to keep you cosy. If you're traveling for business, bring your suit, as the office will likely be freezing.

Culture

Singapore is sometimes referred to as "The Fine City". Some behaviours that may be commonplace or slightly rude somewhere else, are prohibited by law in this city-state and punishable by a fee. For example, under the Singapore law, you could face a hefty fine or even land up in jail if you get caught selling or importing chewing gum! Singapore's high standards of cleanliness influence the way the locals dress. The locals prefer to dress in neat, smart casual clothing and frown on scruffiness. While the older generation dresses conservatively, the younger crowd is more relaxed and casual. Singaporean women tend to look elegant and classic. Include a dress in a simple and flattering cut, which can take you from day to evening. Bring skirts you can wear casually during the day and dress up with heels and a nice blouse at night.

There is an unwritten etiquette that one must not wear revealing clothes. Unless you want to attract attention, leave tiny shorts, and crop tops at home. Dress modestly when visiting temples, mosques, or churches by covering your shoulders and

Singapore

knees. Bring a pashmina or shawl to double as a source of warmth or extra cover.

Given the humidity and rain, spending your entire day in flip-flops is perfectly normal. You will see locals and tourists wearing flip-flops everywhere — whether in malls, on the MRT, at attractions, or strolling through the gardens. However, some upscale restaurants and bars have a strict dress code and a no-flip-flop policy. So, bring a nice pair of heels or wedges for your evening outfits.

Comfort

Due to the hot and humid weather, comfort is paramount when packing for Singapore. Opt for loose-fitting, lightweight, and moisture-wicking clothing to stay fresh and comfortable throughout the day. You may find yourself changing clothes up to three times a day, so choose thin fabrics that can be washed and dried quickly. While it is perfectly acceptable to wear jeans, you will probably be too hot. Jeans are also difficult to dry if you get caught in a shower.

Colour scheme

While no prescribed colour scheme exists, avoid white and light colours, which may become transparent in the rain. Stay away from white or pastel-coloured shoes. They will be much browner by the end of your trip! Singaporeans tend to embrace bright and bold colours, especially during festive occasions. Incorporating vibrant colours such as red, orange, gold, and emerald green into your outfits can be a fun way to blend in with the festive atmosphere.

Singapore

Textures

The rule of thumb is to keep clothing light, breathable, and comfortable. Light and breathable fabrics like cotton, linen, silk, and chambray are ideal for Singapore's climate. These fabrics allow for better airflow and help you stay comfortable in the heat. Alternatively, opt for moisture-wicking synthetic blends. In general, avoid soft materials and suede, as these will get ruined in the rain showers.

Must-haves

Here are some essential items for your trip to Singapore:

Clothing

- T-shirts and tank tops
- Loose shirt
- Lightweight, airy dresses
- Loose cotton or linen shorts
- Skirt
- Elegant dress
- Cardigan or blazer
- Swimwear and cover-up
- Pair of leggings or biker shorts (if hiking)
- Lightweight rain jacket

Singapore

Footwear

- Flip-flops
- Comfortable and lightweight shoes or sandals
- Waterproof trainers (if hiking)
- Dress shoes for upscale venues

Accessories

- Shawl or pashmina
- Umbrella
- Small backpack or crossbody bag
- Sunglasses
- Sunhat or cap

Singapore

Good to have

Consider taking a linen co-ord set or a tailored suit that you can wear together or mix and match with other items. A compact and portable fan can be helpful to keep invigorated when exploring the city. A reusable water bottle is also a good idea to stay hydrated throughout the day. Also, remember that smoking is banned in most public places. Bringing cigarettes and e-cigarettes into the country is illegal. So is gum. It is said that you can buy gum from dentists or pharmacists for medical reasons, but why take the risk? If you are a smoker, pack alternatives such as patches. Finally, if you're taking a professional camera, include a rain cover, especially if you're visiting during the monsoon season. Consider packing a small microfiber towel to bring along when you explore.

Traditional fashion elements to consider

While Singapore is a modern and cosmopolitan city, you can still find elements of traditional fashion in various cultural neighbourhoods. Consider exploring the vibrant Little India or Chinatown districts to find traditional clothing and accessories like *saris*, *cheongsams*, or *batik* prints. Incorporating some of these traditional elements into your travel capsule can add a beautiful touch of traditional style to your looks. Also, Singapore is home to many talented local designers. Head to Orchard Road and treat yourself to a special fashion memento from one of the local contemporary designers. For inspiration on what to wear to Singapore, check out our Singapore Collection on Pinterest. Search for @travelwithstylecollection in the home search bar to find our curated boards.

Singapore

NOTES

Singapore

Skiing

If you are new to skiing, figuring out what to wear can be daunting. Picking the right clothes can make or break your experience and affect your desire to ski. The key is finding skiing apparel that will be warm (but not too warm) and will give you a full range of movement. The good news is the days are gone when skiwear made you look like a duvet! Now, skiwear isn't just practical, it is chic too. Yes, getting the right gear for skiing requires some investment. Skiing clothes are costly, but a proper set lasts many powdery seasons. Here's what you need to know when packing for skiing.

Climate

When travelling to the mountains, the weather will vary depending on the location and season. Know what the forecasted temperatures are for the week and if it's supposed to be sunny or snowy. Also, it's good to check the moisture content of the snow where you will be skiing. If the snow tends to be drier because of cooler temperatures, consider a jacket with a slightly lower waterproof rating but more insulation to protect from the cold air. The ski jackets and pants will indicate their breathability and insulation ratings. Always check them before purchasing. When I first started skiing, I made the mistake of bringing a very warm down jacket on a trip to Chamonix. The weather on the slopes was absolutely glorious, with sunny skies and clear conditions. However, as the morning went on, I began to sweat profusely because my jacket lacked proper ventilation and was far too warm for the conditions. This prompted me to invest in a proper ski jacket that was better suited for skiing in the Alps.

Culture

While most ski resorts have a relaxed and laid-back vibe, others can turn into a real-life couture fashion show, complete with fur coats, feather boas, and enough carats to blind a man. I recommend doing a bit of research on Instagram to figure out what is the norm at your destination. In either case, avoid wearing jeans. Jeans will leave you cold, wet, and looking out of place on the slopes. They are a major fashion faux pas in ski fashion.

If you want to achieve that chic ski style, choose a belted ski jacket with a feminine silhouette, a good quality turtleneck sweater, and skinny-fit ski pants. Alternatively, go for the elegant and retro-inspired colour-blocked ski suit.

Each country may have its take on ski etiquette and safety, so it's better to err on the side of caution. I recommend investing in a ski helmet to prevent any severe injuries. Accidents do happen, and

Skiing

safety is more important than looking cute. Bring a beany or furry ski headband to change into for the après-ski.

Most ski resorts have a bumping après-ski scene. Après-ski refers to all the relaxing, eating, and dancing you get to enjoy with your friends after a day on the slopes. For the après-ski, ditch your skis, add a fine-knit turtleneck sweater with black leggings or fitted trousers, a cosy faux-fur coat, a pair of shearling boots, and a cute furry handbag. It's worth noting that in some high-end resorts, women dress up when going out in the evenings. Do your research and pack accordingly.

Comfort

Invest in high-quality ski apparel that shields you from the cold and snow but is breathable and functional.

Layering is essential to regulate body temperature. Bring a base layer, a mid-layer, and a waterproof and windproof layer. It's common to start the day all bundled up, then shed a layer after a few hours when the sun comes out.

You will want something highly breathable, quick-drying, and moisture-wicking for your base layer. If you don't want to buy a pair of thermal leggings, you can wear yoga pants or gym leggings. For your mid layer, you can get creative and find something that fits your personal style. The primary purpose of this layer is a little extra warmth. This could be a light fleece sweatshirt, a wool sweater, or a turtleneck.

Your ski pants and ski jacket (or suit) should be the most water-proof and windproof layer, especially if you're a newbie and fall a lot! Pay attention to the manufacturer's ratings of the waterproofing and

Skiing

breathability of the item to ensure you get the right gear. Also, they must have good ventilation, such as thigh zips, for those warmer days or once your heart rate increases. A good ski jacket will have lots of pockets, an inner gasket that snugs around your waist and cuff gaskets to prevent snow from creeping inside during a fall, "pit zips" or vents, and a ski pass pocket in the sleeve.

You will want to bring several pairs of high-quality ski socks. They should be knee-high or at least as tall as the cuff of your ski boots. There's nothing worse than having a short sock that creases in your boot, causing lots of discomfort throughout the day.

While you won't be wearing shoes on the slopes, they are crucial once the ski boots are off. I am a massive fan of the Moon Boots. The moon landings inspired the original Moon Boots, which have now become the epitome of the slopes. They are the most comfortable thing to put your feet into after hours of skiing! However, if you prefer a more elegant, streamlined look, opt for waterproof snow boots from brands like Sorel.

Colour scheme

The colours you choose to wear on the slopes are entirely your choice. Classic black and white is popular, as well as reds, yellows, and blues. Many designers now create funky block colour combinations and prints. However, white and black can blend into the surroundings and make you less visible. This can cause danger in case of fog or avalanches. If you're a beginner, it's better to dress in bright colours to ensure you're highly visible on the slopes.

Textures

Fabrics with excellent thermal insulation properties are essential. For base layers, look for moisture-wicking and thermal materials like merino wool and technical blends. The best ski socks are made from merino wool or a blend of wool with nylon or polyester. The second layer can be wool, fleece, or a technical blend. The outer layer should be a synthetic waterproof and windproof material or shell.

Must-haves

Some must-have items for a skiing trip include:

Clothing

- Thermal underwear (tops and bottoms)
- Several pairs of ski socks
- Several wool or fleece sweaters
- Ski pants or bibs
- Insulated trousers
- Waterproof and/or windproof ski jacket
- Warm, cosy clothing for lounging
- Elegant eveningwear (if required)
- Swimsuit (if hot tub, pool, or sauna is available)

Skiing

Footwear

- Snow boots for walking around the resort
- Comfortable footwear for après-ski
- Dress shoes for formal occasions (if required)
- Slippers

Accessories

- Ski gloves
- Warm gloves or mittens for walking around the report
- Beanie or ski headband
- Warm scarf
- Ski helmet
- Ski goggles
- Small backpack to carry gear and snacks
- Sunglasses

Skiing

Good to have

Consider bringing a neck gaiter or a balaclava for extra warmth. I personally like to tie a small silk scarf around the back of my head instead. You can include a pair of warm leather gloves to keep you cosy and chic at the après-ski. Pack a small backpack to carry a refillable water bottle, a power bank, and a lip balm to keep your lips from chapping in the cold.

Traditional fashion elements to consider

While I can't include all the traditional fashion elements from any specific country in this section, I'd like to mention a few things that have become iconic on slopes around the world. These include Moon Boots, bright-shell ski suits inspired by the 80s ski fashion, the Fair Isle sweater, Christmas-style sweaters, turtlenecks, and furry accessories. Experiment and incorporate them into your outfits to work out your personal on- and off-the-slopes style! For inspiration on what to wear to your ski holiday, check out our Skiing Collection on Pinterest. Search for @travelwithstylecollection in the home search bar to find our curated boards.

Skiing

NOTES

_____

_____

_____

_____

_____

_____

_____

_____

_____

_____

_____

_____

_____

_____

_____

_____

Skiing

Tokyo

Tokyo is rich in culture and tradition. It's a destination where ancient temples blend effortlessly with contemporary architecture and cutting-edge technology. This sprawling metropolis offers incredible experiences, from futuristic technology and bustling shopping districts like Shibuya to serene temples and historic neighbourhoods like Asakusa. You can savour delicious Japanese cuisine, immerse yourself in a rich cultural heritage, explore beautiful parks and gardens, and shop for the latest fashion in trendy districts. Japan has four distinct and spectacular seasons, with drastic weather changes. If you plan to stay in Tokyo, create a capsule that reflects its urban vibe. If you are venturing to the mountains or the countryside, opt for a warmer wardrobe, especially in the winter.

Climate

Tokyo experiences four distinct seasons. Summers are hot and humid, with temperatures around 25-30°C (77-86°F). Winters are cold and dry, ranging from 0-10°C (32-50°F). Spring brings mild temperatures and cherry blossoms, while autumn is pleasant, with temperatures around 15-20°C (59-68°F). The time of year you plan to visit will significantly influence your wardrobe.

Spring is a popular time to visit Japan, but the weather can vary. March and early April are much cooler than May. The morning and evening temperatures are around 5°C (41°F), reaching around 13°C (55°F) during the day. So, if you are travelling to Japan in March and early April, I suggest packing gloves, a scarf, and a waterproof jacket. By mid-April, the weather begins to clear up and temperatures rise. Days are mostly mild, with temperatures at 19°C (66°F). However, there is a chill in the air during the early mornings and evenings, so come prepared with plenty of warm layers. May brings balmy temperatures of 23°C (74°F) during the day and 15°C (59°F) in the mornings and evenings.

Tokyo

Culture

The Japanese pride themselves on being refined and orderly, which translates into their dress. In Tokyo, the older generation tends to dress more conservatively, while the younger generations have a more eclectic and daring style. Nonetheless, the wild fashion statements in Harajuku aren't typical for everyday wear. Respectful, modest clothing and proper etiquette are highly valued. In big cities like Tokyo, you will see streetwear and trendy sneakers, but the overall style leans towards smart casual. Messy clothing is frowned upon, especially when visiting temples, shrines, and traditional restaurants where guests should appear polished. Japanese style is about being minimalistic, clean, and well put together. Avoid wearing clothing with offensive prints or slogans.

It's also important to avoid revealing clothing that exposes your shoulders and chest (or knees when visiting temples). Opt for loose trousers or an elegant midi skirt paired with a T-shirt or blouse. Also, wearing shoes inside a traditional Japanese home or a temple is generally considered rude. You will be asked to take them off at the entrance. So, bring extra socks to slip on, and make sure they don't have any holes!

If you're travelling for business, ensure you have a suit. You can wear trousers or a knee-length skirt-suit with dark-coloured tights. Avoid an all-black look, as this is associated with funerals. Revealing and sleeveless blouses are not advisable for business attire. Be wary of showing cleavage in a business setting, it's often frowned upon. Opt for a pair of heels in a neutral colour, minimalist jewellery, and neutral makeup.

If you plan to visit the public baths known as *onsen*, remember that tattoos are still associated with Japan's *Yakuza* (mafia). Be sure to hide them with bandages to avoid being turned away. Swimwear is generally banned in *onsens*, although this rule has a few exceptions. Remember that your hair should never touch the water, so bring something to tie it up.

Tokyo

Comfort

Layering is vital for staying comfortable, as the weather can vary significantly throughout the day. Wear thermal layers in winter months. In winter, it's common for snow to fall. Temperatures can drop in the evenings, and it feels much colder when the wind picks up. Be prepared with thermal tops, leggings, warm clothes, winter accessories, and water-resistant shoes. It is worth noting that most restaurants, bars, and hotels have heating during winter, so it's wise to include layers that you can peel off easily. On the contrary, the summer heat can be oppressive, and air-conditioning is not available everywhere. Pack lightweight, breathable fabrics in summer.

With a ban on private cars, Tokyo requires a lot of walking and commuting. Many streets in the city's historic areas are paved with cobblestones and many temples have hilly landscapes. I can't emphasise enough how crucial it is to take comfortable walking shoes. All the better if you can easily slip them on and off for visits to temples or restaurants where you're required to remove them. Sandals are typical during the summer, late spring, and early fall, weather permitting. Simple white trainers work well year-round. If visiting in winter, bring along closed, water-resistant shoes with thick soles or boots. Include a pair of neutral-coloured heels to change into in the evenings.

Colour Scheme

Neutral colours like black, grey, navy, and white are versatile and widespread in Tokyo. Neutral-coloured items that go well with your outer layers make it easy to assimilate into Japanese culture. Bright colours, like pastels, are more appropriate in spring, a time of renewal and freshness. Elevate your looks with funky accessories that nod to Japanese traditional fashion or the sleek high-tech aesthetic. Incorporate pieces with metallic textures, such as silver or chrome, or pixelated prints and holographic patterns. Make this your statement piece and mix it with more basic items to create balanced looks.

Tokyo

Textures

Select your fabrics based on the season. Summers in Japan can be sweltering, with high humidity and limited air-conditioning indoors. Choose light and breathable fabrics like cotton, linen, and rayon. In winter, bring moisture-wicking thermal base tops and leggings, woollen jumpers, fleece or down vest, and a warm, water-resistant jacket. A shearling or down jacket will do the trick. Spring and fall require layering. Opt for a natural base layer made of cotton and add warmer pieces from wool and fabric blends as the second and third layers. Your outer layer should be wind-proof and water-resistant. If you're feeling adventurous, experiment with futuristic textures such as mesh, organza, PVC or Neoprene for a sci-fi-inspired look. Embrace the world of 3D printing by integrating accessories crafted with this cutting-edge technology. You can find an array of options, from 3D-printed jewellery and eyewear to garments.

Must-Haves

Below is a list of what you should pack for your trip to Japan, depending on your travel season.

Winter

Clothing
▪ Thermal tops
▪ Thermal leggings or warm tights
▪ Wool blend trousers

Tokyo

- Dark jeans
- Long knitted dress
- Long-sleeve tops
- Blouses
- Sweaters or fleece
- Warm coat or down jacket

Footwear

- Warm, waterproof boots
- Pair of dressy boots

Accessories

- Gloves or mittens
- Warm scarf
- Warm hat or earmuffs
- Cross-body bag
- Sunglasses
- Umbrella

Tokyo

Spring / Autumn

Clothing

- Thermal top (early spring and late autumn)
- T-shirts

- Long-sleeve tops and shirts
- Blouse
- Tailored trousers
- Jeans
- Midi skirt
- Midi dress
- Light sweaters or cardigans
- Raincoat or trench
- Leather or denim jacket

Footwear

- Comfortable sandals
- Comfortable sneakers
- Comfortable, waterproof boots (early spring and late autumn)

Accessories

- Umbrella
- Cross-body bag
- Scarf
- Sunglasses

Tokyo

Summer

Clothing

- T-shirts and sleeveless blouses
- Light and airy midi dress
- Capri shorts
- Skirt
- Loose shirt
- Light cardigan
- Light rain jacket (rainy season)

Footwear

- Comfortable sandals
- Waterproof tennis shoes (rainy season)

Accessories

- Umbrella (for unexpected rain or mid-day sun)
- Sunhat or cap
- Sunglasses
- Cross-body bag

Tokyo

Good to Haves

At the time of publishing this book, masks remain a requirement in most public places. Bring your reusable face mask or enough disposable ones to get you through the first few days of the trip. Consider taking a reusable shopping bag for your shopping and souvenirs. When travelling in the summer, having a reusable water bottle and a hand-held fan is helpful to keep chilled in the heat. Also, bring blotting paper to dab away excess sweat and oil without ruining your make up. When travelling in winter, consider taking disposable heating pads. If you plan to visit during the rainy season, consider taking a waterproof bag made from water-resistant faux leather.

Traditional Fashion Elements to Consider

Traditional Japanese clothing is a must-try for any visitor. We've all heard of the *Kimono*, but did you know there are over thirty pieces of traditional Japanese clothing? Many of them are reserved for ceremonies and special occasions. However, there are items you can certainly wear on your next trip to Japan.

Don a traditional *Kimono* or *yukata* for your temple visits or traditional tea ceremony. Kimonos are usually made from silk. The *yukatas* are their casual counterpart, typically made from cotton or linen, making them perfect for warmer months. Your hosts at a *Ryokan* (a traditional Japanese inn) will typically provide *yukatas* for their guests. You can wear these indoors and on temple visits.

Samue is a matching loose trousers and top set, typically in blue or green. Created by Japanese Zen Buddhist clergy, Samue makes for great loungewear. They are also adjustable, so they can grow and shrink as we all inevitably do. A similar matching set called *Jinbei* has short sleeves and a half pant, making it perfect for the summer months.

Tokyo

Another gorgeous item to incorporate into your looks is an *Obi*. It is the wide sash that keeps the *Kimono* together. Obis come as minimalist or flamboyant as you like, so you can definitely find one to match your style. It's a hugely flattering accessory that will elevate your looks and make a gorgeous souvenir.

If travelling in winter, consider incorporating the iconic *Hanten* jacket. The Hanten is a short, cotton-padded coat with a tailored collar. Its mixture of Japanese minimalism and practicality makes it a welcome addition to the modern wardrobe.

Kanzashi is an ornate hairpin or hair comb made from metal or tortoiseshell. It's decorated with flowers, colourful embellishments, or jewellery. Wear a *Kanzashi* to add traditional elegance to your evening outfits.

Finally, Tokyo is home to many internationally recognized brands like Uniqlo, Miyake, Kawakubo, and Yamamoto. Explore the shops at Shibuya, Aoyama, Daikanyama, and Ginza to find unique pieces from home-grown designers. For inspiration on what to wear to Tokyo, check out our Tokyo Collection on Pinterest. Search for @travelwithstylecollection in the home search bar to find our curated boards.

Tokyo

NOTES

Tokyo

PART 3

Packing FAQs:
Tips from a Savvy Traveller

How do I pack efficiently and maximise space in my luggage?

First, remember that packing efficiently isn't about squeezing more clothes into a suitcase. It's about being smart about what you pack. Choose versatile items that can be mixed to create multiple outfits and be worn on numerous occasions. (See 'Chapter 2: Building Your Travel Capsule: Star with the Basics'.)

Your method of packing dramatically influences how much you can fit into your suitcase, and what your clothes will look like on the other end. There's a widespread belief that rolling your clothes instead of folding them saves space and minimises wrinkles. This is true if you're packing a backpack, a weekend bag, or using packing cubes. However, if you're travelling with a suitcase (and not using cubes), there's a better way. My father shared this little trick when I was a teenager, and I'm pleased to pass it on to you.

Instead of folding, lay each item flat on top of the other. Start with heavier items, such as trousers and jeans. Then layer lighter items such as skirts, blouses, and tops. Fold long trousers or dresses once in the middle and lay flat. Lay blouses flat and fold in the sleeves at the seam line. Laying your clothes flat allows you to maximise the space and keep the items from creasing. Fill the suitcase up evenly. Lay clothes next to each other, so that your clothes are level.

Once you're done packing your clothes, top off your suitcase with your shoes, toiletries, accessories, and underwear. I always use dust bags for my shoes and handbags. I suggest designating a specific dust bag or a packing cube for your underwear. This saves you any embarrassment in case you need to open your suitcase at the airport.

You can also use compression packing cubes to organise and compress your clothing, making it easier to find what you need. This works well if you're planning a multi-city trip and will be changing hotels every few nights. You can organise your clothes into separate cubes for each location, climate, or activity. Operating this way will save you a ton of time packing and unpacking in each hotel.

Consider wearing bulkier items (such as jackets or boots) during transit to free up space in your luggage. Hats, scarves, and large totes should also come with you in the plane cabin. Taking a large tote on the flight allows you to maximise your baggage allowance and take any essentials such as travel-size toiletries, chargers, iPads, kindle, or books in your personal items. Use your hand luggage to pack essentials such as pyjamas, your toothbrush, fresh underwear, and a change of clothes. This is especially important if you have a connecting flight, in case your luggage misses your connection.

What essentials should I include in my travel packing list?

Apart from destination-specific suggestions (which you can find in Part 2 of this book), here's a complete list of essential items you can include:

Clothing

- Tops (t-shirts, blouses, shirts)
- Bottoms (trousers, shorts, skirts)
- Dresses or jumpsuits
- Outerwear (jackets, sweaters)
- Underwear and socks
- Sleepwear
- Swimsuit (if applicable)

FAQs

- Activewear
- Loungewear

Footwear

- Comfortable walking shoes
- Sandals or flip-flops
- Dress shoes (if needed)
- Hiking boots (if needed)
- Trainers or sneakers (if needed)

Accessories

- Hat or cap
- Sunglasses
- Scarves or wraps
- Belts
- Jewellery
- Day bag
- Evening bag

FAQs

Toiletries

- Toothbrush and toothpaste
- Haircare essentials
- Sunscreen
- Insect repellent

- Hand sanitiser
- Makeup
- Hairbrush
- Skin care essentials

Medications and First Aid

- Prescription medications
- Over-the-counter medications (pain relievers, motion sickness pills, etc.)
- First aid kit (band-aids, antiseptic etc.)

Electronics

- Phone and charger
- Laptop or tablet and charger
- Power bank
- Camera and accessories
- Travel adapters and converters

Documents

- Passport and visa (if needed)
- Travel itinerary and tickets
- Hotel and accommodation confirmations
- Travel insurance information
- Driver's license (if renting a car)

FAQs

Miscellaneous

- Travel pillow and eye mask
- Microfiber towel (if applicable)
- Umbrella
- Reusable water bottle
- Books or e-reader
- Headphones

Money and Essentials

- Cash
- credit cards
- Wallet
- Local Sim card

It's also a good idea to check if there are any specific items you'll need based on the local customs, regulations, or cultural norms of the place you're visiting.

You can find a printable version of this checklist on our website: www.travelwithstyle.co

How to avoid overpacking?

Start by planning your outfits for your trip, and keep in mind the activities and weather conditions. Embrace the concept of capsule

FAQs

dressing, selecting a limited number of items that work well together. Stick to a colour scheme to ensure coordination. Be ruthless when editing your selections and eliminate items that are redundant. Lastly, remember that you can always do laundry or repeat outfits if necessary. The more I travelled with this philosophy in mind, the more comfortable I became with the idea of selecting a few versatile pieces that complement each other. Like anything else, it's a matter of practice.

How do I pack for destinations with micro-climates and varied weather conditions?

Start by researching the weather patterns of your destination during the specific time you'll be traveling. Then, select clothing items that can be easily layered to adapt to these conditions. Opt for light-weight, moisture-wicking fabrics for warmer days and include items like shorts, dresses, and breathable tops. Pack a light sweatshirt or hoodie for colder days. Bring a waterproof and windproof jacket for unexpected rain showers and gusts of wind. Include a scarf or pash-mina and a hat to add style and functionality to your looks. Don't forget comfortable walking shoes that can handle various terrains and weather conditions. Focus on a colour scheme that allows to mix-and-match items, making it easier to create different looks.

For example, we're currently planning a trip to Sri Lanka during the Christmas holidays. Highland regions like Nuwara Eliya (known for tea cultivation) get quite chilly in December. On the other hand, coastal areas in the south, such as Yala National Park and Unawatuna, have much warmer weather. I'll be packing a few long, breathable dresses, long trousers, long-sleeve shirt, T-shirts, a

FAQs

warm jumper, and a jacket for this trip. In terms of footwear, I'll be bringing flip-flops for the beach and my Dr Martens boots for hiking, walking around the tea plantations, and going on a safari in the national park. Of course, I never travel without my hat and a pashmina, which can serve as a scarf on chilly days or a cover-up when visiting temples.

What type of luggage is best for my travel needs: suitcase, backpack, or carry-on?

The type of luggage that's best for your travel needs depends on a few factors, such as the length of your trip, the destinations you'll be visiting, and your personal preferences. My top choice is a hard-shell suitcase since I often take longer journeys and prefer the security of a combination lock. My close second is a backpack with multiple compartments. It's perfect for shorter getaways, helping me stay organized throughout my travels. Here's a breakdown to help you decide.

SUITCASE

Best for longer trips, business travel, and organised packing.

Pros: Offers ample space, organised compartments, wheels for easy manoeuvrability, ideal for formal attire.

Cons: It may be too bulky for off-the-beaten-path exploration. Some safari routes won't accept a suitcase on the small Cessna planes. Inconvenient for frequent short distance travelling within the destination. It can be challenging on uneven terrain such as sandy beaches, cobblestones, or dirt roads.

Destinations: Business conferences, resort vacations, long city trips.

BACKPACK

Best for shorter trips, urban exploration, backpacking, and hands-free travel.

Pros: Lightweight, great for short-distance travel within the destination, passes for a carry-on for flights, versatile for different terrains, and hands-free.

Cons: Limited packing space, usually less organised compartments, not ideal for formal or evening attire.

Destinations: Hiking trips, backpacking adventures, island hopping, exploring cities with cobblestone streets.

CARRY-ON

Best for short trips and travelling light.

Pros: Saves time at the airport, easy to manoeuvre, less risk of lost luggage.

Cons: Limited space, will not accommodate larger or bulkier items.

Destinations: Weekend getaways, quick city breaks, and business trips.

WEEKENDER BAG

Best for short trips, weekend getaways, light packers, safari, or sailing.

Pros: Compact yet spacious enough for essentials, easy to carry, folds away easily.

Cons: Limited space for longer trips, few organisational features.

Destinations: Weekend escapes, beach trips, road trips, overnight visits, desert, safari.

FAQs

How many outfits should I pack for my trip?

The number of outfits you should pack for your trip depends on several factors, including the length of your trip, the type of activities you'll engage in, and your style. A general guideline is to plan for a mix of versatile pieces that can be mixed to create multiple looks. Drawing from my experience of everything from packing for quick work trips to extended overseas stays lasting from three to six months, here's a breakdown based on trip durations.

WEEKEND GETAWAY (2-3 DAYS)

For a short weekend trip, aim for three to four looks. Pack a mix of casual and slightly dressier options, based on your planned activities.

WEEK-LONG TRIP (7 DAYS)

For a week-long adventure, prepare around ten to fourteen looks. Include tops, bottoms, and dresses that can be layered and interchanged easily. Opt for accessories that can work with multiple outfits, so you can create more looks through styling, instead of packing more clothes.

TWO-WEEK VACATION (14 DAYS)

Plan for approximately twenty outfits. Choose pieces that you can mix and match to create multiple looks — bonus points for looks you can reutilize for several occasions. Pick out accessories that work with multiple outfits.

FAQs

Extended Travel (3 weeks or more)

For longer trips, aim for over twenty-five outfits. Prioritise mix-and-match items that work well together to ensure you have a wide variety without overpacking. Choose accessories that work with multiple looks and occasions. Pack a few statement accessories that can transform a basic outfit into something special. You are likely to shop for additional items during your trip, so don't stress about not having enough clothes.

Remember to use laundry facilities at your destination or plan to do some handwashing if needed.

How do I prevent wrinkles and keep my clothes looking fresh during travel?

Here are a few handy tips to help you arrive at your destination with outfits ready to wear and to keep them fresh during your trip.

Don't Fold: Instead of folding your clothes, lie them flat or roll them up tightly if using packing cubes. This minimises creases and takes up less space. If folding is necessary, fold clothes along the natural seams to minimise creases.

Use Packing Cubes: Invest in packing cubes to organise your clothing. Separating items into cubes prevents friction and helps maintain their condition.

Pack Items Inside Out: Turn delicate or printed items inside out to protect the outer surface from abrasion.

FAQs

Pack Heavy Items at the Bottom: Place heavier items, like jeans, at the bottom of your suitcase to reduce pressure on lighter garments.

Hang-Up Garments: If you're staying in a hotel with a wardrobe, use the hangers provided to hang clothes as soon as you check-in.

Travel Steamers: Portable travel steamers are compact and efficient for quickly removing wrinkles. Steam from the shower can also help release wrinkles.

Wrinkle-Release Spray: Pack a travel-sized, wrinkle-release spray. A quick spritz and gentle tugging can help smooth out minor wrinkles.

Limit Overpacking: Avoid cramming your suitcase, overpacking can lead to more wrinkles. Leave some space for items to breathe.

What do I do with the clothes I buy for my vacation and during my travels?

When shopping before or during your travels, align your purchases with your personal style and long-term wardrobe needs. Resist the temptation of impulse buying cute but ultimately impractical items or buying things just because they seem like a bargain. Focus on acquiring pieces that can integrate into your daily wardrobe or can be helpful in future holiday ensembles. Nevertheless, sometimes the temptation is just too big! If it becomes clear that an item you bought doesn't quite fit these criteria, consider passing it along to a local charity shop, a clothing bank, or your new local friends before

FAQs

heading home. This mindful approach prevents clutter back home and extends the life of your travel finds.

On the other hand, if you will be returning to this destination, consider bringing these items with you and storing them for your next visit. This is what I did when I spent several months living in Bali and ended up accumulating various beach-friendly outfits that were not appropriate for the city. Knowing I would return, I donated the items I didn't adore to charity and kept my favourite pieces in storage for my next trip.

A Final Word from the Author

As you turn the final page, I hope you feel empowered and inspired to embark on your own style-filled journeys around the world. Remember that style isn't just about clothing. It's a reflection of your unique personality, a way to express yourself, and a means to connect with the cultures you experience. Whether you're exploring bustling cities, tranquil beaches, or majestic mountains, your travel capsule is your canvas to create unforgettable memories and capture the essence of each destination.

As you pack your bags and step into new adventures, may these pages serve as your trusty guide, helping you craft the perfect travel capsule, choose the right colours and textures, and embrace the fashion traditions that make each place truly extraordinary. Cherish the moments standing before a mirror, with an outfit that embodies the local spirit, knowing that you've mastered the art of curating your own unique travel style.

Wherever your wanderlust takes you next, remember fashion is not just about looking good. It's also about feeling confident and comfortable in your skin. Your journey is an ever-evolving one. As you explore the world with an open heart and a stylish capsule, you'll discover the memories you create are the most fashionable accessory of all.

If you've enjoyed this book and found the tips and insights useful, please leave it a review on Amazon and Goodreads. Your feedback means the world to me, and it can help others in making the right choice when considering this book. Thank you for contributing to our community of explorers!

Beyond this book, there are several resources for you to explore. Our website www.travelwithstyle.co is a hub where you can download packing checklists for each destination. Our curated Pinterest boards on @travelwithstylecollection provide inspiration for the destinations covered in this book. Our personal stylist keeps the boards updated and shares finds from online shops, so you don't have to spend hours searching for the right pieces.

You can also join our community of fellow stylish travellers on Instagram: @travelwithstylebook. We hold regular live broadcasts with stylists, designers, and bloggers from all around the world. So, you'll be able to tap into their knowledge and experience. We also love to see what looks you create for your trips and regularly share our community's looks. Use the hashtag #itravelwithstyle and share your posts to our DM to showcase your travel outfits. I can't wait to see the looks you create!

Here's to your travels, your style, and the remarkable journey that lies ahead. Bon voyage and happy exploring!

With love,
Anastasia